✓

Natti S. Rao

Design Formulas for Plastics Engineers

with 90 Figures

Hanser Publishers, Munich Vienna New York

Distributed in the United States of America and Canada
by Oxford University Press, New York

Distributed in USA and in Canada by
Oxford University Press
200 Madison Avenue, New York, N.Y. 10016

Distributed in all other countries by
Carl Hanser Verlag
Kolbergerstrasse 22
D-8000 München 80

The use of general descriptive names, trademarks, etc. in this publication, even if the former are not especially identified, is not to be taken as a sign that such names, as understood by the Trade Marks and Merchandise Marks Act, may accordingly be used freely by anyone.

While the advice and information in this book are believed to be true and accurate at the date of going to press, neither the authors nor the editors nor the publisher can accept any legal responsibility for any errors or omissions that may be made. The publisher makes no warranty, express or implied, with respect to the material contained herein.

Library of Congress Cataloging-in-Publication Data

Rao, Natti S.:

Design formulas for plastics engineers / Natti S. Rao.
p.   cm.
Includes bibliographical references and index.
ISBN 0-19-520908-7 (Oxford University Press)
1. Plastics.   I. Title.
TP1140.R36   1991   91-71069
668.4--dc20   CIP

CIP-Titelaufnahme der Deutschen Bibliothek

Rao, Natti S.:

Design formulas for plastic engineers / Natti S. Rao. – Munich ; Vienna ; New York : Hanser ; New York : Oxford Univ. Pr., 1991
Einheitssacht.: Formeln der Kunststofftechnik ⟨engl.⟩
ISBN 3-446-15687-9

ISBN 3-446-15687-9   Carl Hanser Verlag, Munich, Vienna, New York
ISBN 0-19-520908-7   Oxford University Press

Contents

1   Preface

Designing machines and dies is done to-day to a large extent with the help of computer programs. However, the predictions of these programs do not always agree with the practical results, so that there is a need to improve the underlying mathematical models. Therefore a knowledge of the formulas, on which the models are based and the limits of their applicability is necessary, if one wants to develop a new program or improve one already in use.

The plastics engineer has often to deal with different fields of engineering. The search for the appropriate equations in the various fields concerned can be time-consuming. A collection of formulas from the relevant fields, as given in this book, makes it easier to write one's own program or to make changes in an existing program, in order to obtain a better fit with the experiments.

It is often the case that different equations are given in the literature on plastics technology for one and the same target quantity sought after. The practising engineer is thus at a loss to judge the validity of the equations he comes across in the literature.

During his long years of activity as an R & D engineer in the polymer field at the BASF AG the author tested many a formula published while solving practical problems. This book presents a summary of the important formulas, which the author, in cooperation with the well-known machine manufacturers, successfully applied to solve design and processing problems. However, the book is to be treated more as an attempt to summarise useful formulas than as a handbook.

The formulas are classified according to the fields, rheology, thermodynamics, heat transfer and part design. Each chapter covers the relevant relations in that particular field. A separate chapter is devoted to treat the practical equations for designing extrusion and injection molding equipment. Numerous thoroughly worked-out problems in metric units illustrate the use of the formulas.

The author wishes to express his thanks to his professional colleagues at the BASF AG for fruitful discussions. Thanks are also due to the Professors LANGECKER and ROTHE for the review of manuscript, criticism and suggestions.

2   Formulas of Rheology

One of the most important steps in processing polymers is melting the resin, which is initially in the solid state and forcing the melt through a die of a given shape. During this operation the melt, whose structure plays a key role in determining the quality of the product to be manufactured, undergoes different flow and deformation processes.

The plastics engineer has therefore to deal with the melt rheology, which describes the flow behaviour and deformation of the melt. The theory of elasticity and hydromechanics can be called as frontier fields of rheology, because the former describes the behaviour of ideal elastic solids, where as the latter is concerned with that of ideal viscous fluids.

Ideal elastic solids deform according to Hookean law and ideal viscous fluids obey laws of Newtonian flow. The latter are also denoted as Newtonian fluids. Plastic melts exhibit both viscous and elastic properties.

Thus the design of machines and dies for polymer processing requires quantitative description of the properties related to polymer melt flow. Starting from the relationships for Hookean solids formulas for describing viscous shear flow of the melt are first treated, as far as they are of practical use in designing polymer machinery. This is followed by a summary of expressions for steady and time-dependent viscoelastic behaviour of melts.

2.1   Ideal Solids

The behavior of a polymer subjected to shear or tension can be described by comparing its reaction to external force with that of an ideal elastic solid under load. To characterize ideal solids, first of all it is necessary to define certain quantities as follows [1]:

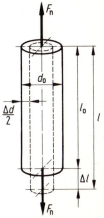

Fig. 2.1   Deformation of a Hookean solid by a tensile stress [1]

The axial force F_n in Fig. 2.1 causes an elongation Δl of the sample of diameter d_0 and length l_0 fixed at one end. Following equations apply for this case:

Engineering strain:

$$\varepsilon' = \frac{\Delta l}{l_0} \qquad (2.1.1)$$

Hencky strain:

$$\varepsilon = \ln\left(\frac{l}{l_0}\right) \qquad (2.1.2)$$

Tensile stress:

$$\sigma_z = \frac{F_n}{A_0} \qquad (2.1.3)$$

Reference area:

$$A_0 = \frac{\pi d_0^2}{4} \qquad (2.1.4)$$

Poisson's ratio:

$$\mu = -\frac{\Delta d/d_0}{\Delta l/l_0} \qquad (2.1.5)$$

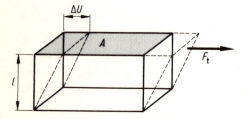

Fig. 2.2   Deformation of a Hookean solid by a shearing stress [1]

Fig. 2.2 shows the influence of a shear force F_t acting on the area A of a rectangular sample and causing the displacement ΔU. The valid expressions are defined by:

Shear strain:

$$\gamma = \frac{\Delta U}{l} \qquad (2.1.6)$$

Shear stress:

$$\tau = \frac{F_t}{A} \qquad (2.1.7)$$

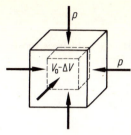

Fig. 2.3   Hookean solid under compression [1]

The isotropic compression due to the pressure acting on all sides of the parallelo-piped shown in Fig. 2.3 is given by the engineering compression ratio $\varkappa$.

$$\varkappa = \frac{\Delta V}{V_0} \tag{2.1.8}$$

Where ΔV is the reduction of volume due to deformation of the body with the original volume V_0.

2.1.1   Hooke's Law

The linear relationships between stress and strain of a Hookean solid are given by [1].

$$\sigma_z = E \cdot \varepsilon' \tag{2.1.9}$$

$$\tau = G \cdot \gamma \tag{2.1.10}$$

$$p = -K \cdot \varkappa \tag{2.1.11}$$

Where E is the modulus of elasticity, G, the shear modulus and K, the bulk modulus. These moduli are constant for a Hookean solid. Furthermore the relationship existing between E, G and K is expressed as [1].

$$E = 2G(1+\mu) = 3K(1-2\mu) \tag{2.1.12}$$

This leads to for an incompressible solid ($K \to \infty$, $\mu \to 0.5$) [1].

$$E = 3G \tag{2.1.13}$$

2.2   Newtonian Fluids

Analogous to the ideal elastic solids there exists a linear relationship between stress and strain in the case of Newtonian fluids.

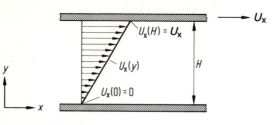

Fig. 2.4   Shear flow

The fluid between the upper plate in Fig. 2.4 moving at a constant velocity U_x and the lower stationary plate experiences a shear stress τ (see also Fig. 2.2).

$$\tau = \frac{F_t}{A}$$

(2.2.1)

The shear or deformation rate of the fluid is equal to

$$\dot{\gamma} = \frac{U_x}{H} = \frac{du}{dy}$$

(2.2.2)

The shear viscosity is defined as

$$\eta = \frac{\tau}{\dot{\gamma}}$$

(2.2.3)

For an extensional flow, which corresponds to the tension test of a Hookean solid, we get

$$\sigma_z = \lambda \cdot \dot{\varepsilon}$$

(2.2.4)

where σ_z = normal stress
        λ = Trouton viscosity
        $\dot{\varepsilon}$ = strain rate

Analogous to Eq. (2.1.13) one obtains

$$\lambda = 3\eta$$

(2.2.5)

2.3   Formulas for Viscous Shear Flow of Polymer Melts

Macromolecular fluids like thermoplastic melts exhibit significant non-Newtonian behaviour. This is noticed in the marked decrease of melt viscosity when the melt is subjected to shear or tension as represented in Fig. 2.5. The flow of melt in the channels of dies and machines of polymer processing machinery is mainly shear flow. Therefore knowledge of the laws of shear flow is necessary for designing machines and dies for polymer processing. For practical applications the following summary of the relationships was found to be useful.

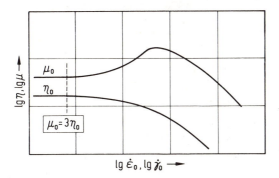

Fig. 2.5   Tensile viscosity and shear viscosity of a polymer melt as a function of strain rate [21]

2.3.1   Apparent Shear Rate

The apparent shear rate for a melt flowing through a capillary is defined as

$$\dot{\gamma}_a = \frac{4\dot{Q}}{\pi R^3}$$

(2.3.1)

where $\dot{Q}$ is the volume flow rate per second and R, the radius of capillary.

2.3.2   Entrance Loss

Another rheological quantity which is of practical importance, is the entrance loss p_c representing the loss of energy of flow at the entrance to a round nozzle. This is correlated empirically by the relation [2]

$$p_c = c \cdot \tau^m$$

(2.3.2)

where c and m are empirical constants and τ, the shear stress. These constants can be determined from the well-known Bagley-curves as shown in Fig. 2.7. The values of these constants are given in Table 2.1 for some of the thermoplastics. The dimensions of shear stress and entrance loss used in the calculation of c and m are in Pa.

Table 2.1   Resin-dependent constants c and m in Eq. (2.3.2) [2]

Polymer	c	m
Polypropylene (Novolen 1120 H)	$2.551 \cdot 10^{-5}$	2.116
Polypropylene (Novolen 1120 L)	$1.463 \cdot 10^{-4}$	1.976
Polypropylene (Novolen 1320 L)	$2.871 \cdot 10^{-7}$	2.469
PE-LD (Lupolen 1800 M)	$1.176 \cdot 10^{-1}$	1.434
PE-LD (Lupolen 1800 S)	$6.984 \cdot 10^{0}$	1.072
PE-LD (Lupolen 1810 D)	$5.688 \cdot 10^{-4}$	1.905
PE-HD (Lupolen 6011 L)	$3.940 \cdot 10^{-2}$	1.399
PE-HD (Lupolen 6041 D)	$1.778 \cdot 10^{0}$	1.187
Polyisobutylene (Oppanol B 10)	$6.401 \cdot 10^{-3}$	1.575
Polyisobutylene (Oppanol B 15)	$1.021 \cdot 10^{-7}$	2.614

2.3.3   True Shear Stress

The flow curves of a particular PE-LD measured with a capillary rheometer are given in Fig. 2.6. The plot shows the apparent shear rate $\dot{\gamma}_a$ as a function of the true shear stress τ at the capillary wall with the melt temperature as a parameter. The entrance loss p_c was obtained from the Bagley plot shown in Fig. 2.7. Thus the true shear stress τ is given by

$$\tau = \frac{p - p_c}{2(L/R)} \tag{2.3.3}$$

where L = length of the capillary
R = radius of the capillary
p = pressure of the melt (see Fig. 2.39).

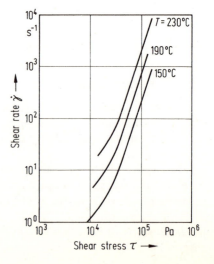

Fig. 2.6   Flow curves of a PE-LD [8]

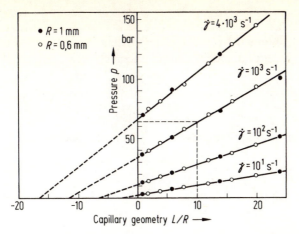

Fig. 2.7   Bagley plots of a polystyrene with the capillary length L and radius R [3]

2.3.4   **Apparent Viscosity**

The apparent viscosity η_a is defined as

$$\eta_a = \frac{\tau}{\dot{\gamma}_a} \tag{2.3.4}$$

and is shown in Fig. 2.8 as a function of shear rate and temperature for a PE-LD.

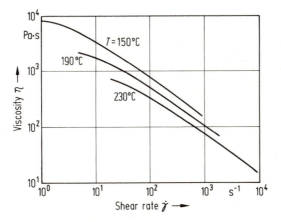

Fig. 2.8   Viscosity functions of a PE-LD [8]

2.3.5   True Shear Rate

The true shear rate $\dot{\gamma}_t$ is obtained from the apparent shear rate by applying the correction for the non-Newtonian behaviour of the melt according to RABINO-WITSCH

$$\dot{\gamma}_t = \left(\frac{n+3}{4}\right)\dot{\gamma}_a \qquad\qquad (2.3.5)$$

The meaning of the power law exponent n is explained in the Section 2.3.7.2.

2.3.6   True Viscosity

The true viscosity η_w is given by

$$\eta_w = \frac{\tau}{\dot{\gamma}_t} \qquad\qquad (2.3.6)$$

In Fig. 2.9 the true and apparent viscosities are plotted as functions of the corresponding shear rates at different temperatures for a polystyrene. As can be seen, the apparent viscosity function is a good approximation for engineering calculations.

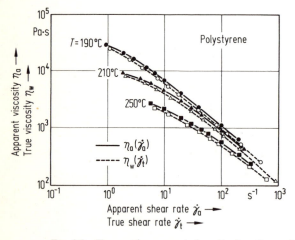

Fig. 2.9   True and apparent viscosity functions of a polystyrene at different temperatures [2]

2.3.7   Empirical Formulas for Apparent Viscosity

Various fluid models have been developed to calculate the apparent shear viscosity η_a [9]. The following sections deal with an important few of these relationships, which are frequently used in design calculations.

2.3.7.1   Hyperbolic Function of PRANDTL and EYRING

The relation between shear rate $\dot{\gamma}_a$ and shear stress τ according to the fluid model of EYRING [4] and PRANDTL [5] can be written as

$$\dot{\gamma}_a = C \sinh(\tau/A) \tag{2.3.7}$$

where C and A are temperature-dependent material constants.

The evaluation of the constants C and A for the flow curve of PE-LD at 190 °C in Fig. 2.10 leads to $C = 4\,s^{-1}$ and $A = 3 \cdot 10^4\,N/m^2$. It can be seen from Fig. 2.10 that the hyperbolic function of PRANDTL and EYRING holds good at low shear rates.

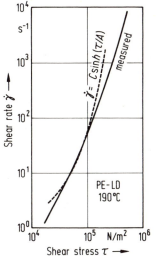

Fig. 2.10   Comparison between measurements and values calculated with Eq. (2.3.7) [8]

2.3.7.2   Power Law of OSTWALD and DE WAELE

The power law of OSTWALD [6] and DE WAELE [7] is easy to use hence widely employed in design work [10]. This relation can be expressed as

$$\dot{\gamma}_a = K \tau^n \tag{2.3.8}$$

or

$$\dot{\gamma}_a = K |\tau^{n-1}| \tau \tag{2.3.9}$$

where K denotes a factor of proportionality and n the power law exponent. Another form of power law often used is

$$\tau = K_R \dot{\gamma}_a^{n_R} \tag{2.3.10}$$

or

$$\tau = K_R \cdot |\dot{\gamma}_a^{n_R - 1}| \dot{\gamma}_a \tag{2.3.11}$$

In this case n_R is the reciprocal of n and $K_R = K^{-n_R}$.

From Eq. (2.3.8) the exponent n can be expressed as

$$n = \frac{d \lg \dot{\gamma}_a}{d \lg \tau} \tag{2.3.12}$$

As shown in Fig. 2.11 in a double log-plot the exponent n represents the local gradient of the curve $\dot{\gamma}_a$ vs τ.

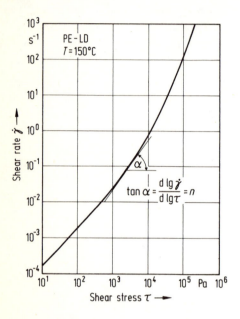

Fig. 2.11   Determination of the power law exponent n in the Eq. (2.3.12)

Furthermore

$$\frac{1}{n} = \frac{d \lg \tau}{d \lg \dot{\gamma}_a} = \frac{d \lg \eta_a + d \lg \dot{\gamma}_a}{d \lg \dot{\gamma}_a} = \frac{d \lg \eta_a}{d \lg \dot{\gamma}_a} + 1 \tag{2.3.13}$$

The values of K and n determined from the flow curve of PE-LD at 190 °C shown in Fig. 2.12 were found to be $K = 1.06 \cdot 10^{-11}$ and $n = 2.57$ [8]. As can be seen from Fig. 2.12 the power law fits the measured values much better than the hyperbolic function of PRANDTL [5] and EYRING [4]. The deviation between the power law and experiment is a result of the assumption that the exponent n is constant throughout the range of shear rates considered, whereas actually n varies with the shear rate. The power law can be extended to consider the effect of temperature on the viscosity as follows:

$$\eta_a = K_{OR} \cdot \exp(-\beta \cdot T) \cdot \dot{\gamma}_a^{n_R - 1} \tag{2.3.14}$$

where K_{OR} = consistency index
         β = temperature coefficient
         T = temperature of melt.

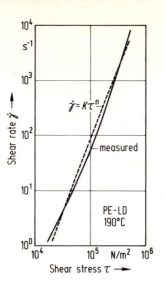

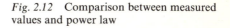

Fig. 2.12 Comparison between measured values and power law

Example:

Following values are given for a PE-LD:

$$n_R = 0.3286$$

$$\beta = 0.00863 \; (°C^{-1})$$

$$K_{OR} = 135990 \; (N \cdot s^{n_R} \cdot m^{-2})$$

The viscosity η_a at $T = 200$ °C and $\gamma_a = 500 \; s^{-1}$ is calculated from Eq. (2.3.14)

$$\eta_a = 373.1 \; Pa \cdot s$$

2.3.7.3 Polynomial of MUENSTEDT

The fourth degree polynomial of MUENSTEDT [2] provides a good fit for the measured values of viscosity. For a definite temperature this is expressed as

$$\lg \eta_a = A_0 + A_1 \lg \dot\gamma_a + A_2 (\lg \dot\gamma_a)^2 + A_3 (\lg \dot\gamma_a)^3 + A_4 (\lg \dot\gamma_a)^4 \qquad (2.3.15)$$

where A_0, A_1, A_2, A_3, A_4 represent resin-dependent constants. These constants can be determined with the help of the program of RAO [10], which is based on multiple linear regression.

This program in its general form fits an equation of the type $y = a_0 + a_1 x_1 + a_2 x_2 + \ldots a_n x_n$ and prints out the coefficients a_0, a_1 and so on for the best fit.

2.3.7.3.1 Shift Factor for Crystalline Polymers

The influence of temperature on viscosity can be taken into acount by the shift factor a_T [2].

For crystalline polymers this can be expressed as

$$a_T = b_1(T_0) \exp(b_2/T) \qquad (2.3.16)$$

where b_1, b_2 = resin-dependent constants
T = melt temperatur (K)
T_0 = reference temperatur (K)

2.3.7.3.2 Shift Factor for Amorphous Polymers

The shift factor a_T for amorphous polymers is derived from the WLF equation and can be written as

$$\lg a_T = \frac{-c_1(T - T_0)}{c_2 + (T - T_0)} \qquad (2.3.17)$$

where c_1, c_2 = resin-dependent constants
T = melt temperature (°C)
T_0 = reference temperature (°C)

The expression for calculating both the effect of temperature and shear rate on viscosity follows from Eq. (2.3.15)

$$\lg \eta_a = \lg a_T + A_0 + A_1 \lg(a_T \dot{\gamma}_a) + A_2 [\lg(a_T \dot{\gamma}_a)]^2$$
$$+ A_3 [\lg(a_T \dot{\gamma}_a)]^3 + A_4 [\lg(a_T \dot{\gamma}_a)]^4 \qquad (2.3.18)$$

With Eq. (2.3.13) we get

$$\frac{1}{n} = 1 + A_1 + 2A_2 \lg(a_T \dot{\gamma}_a) + 3A_3 [\lg(a_T \dot{\gamma}_a)]^2$$
$$+ 4A_4 [\lg(a_T \dot{\gamma}_a)]^3 \qquad (2.3.19)$$

The power law exponent is often required in the design work as a function of shear rate and temperature. Fig. 2.13 illustrates this relationship for a definite PE-LD. The curves shown are computed with Eqns. (2.3.16) and (2.3.19). As can be inferred from Fig. 2.13, the assumption of a constant value for the power law exponent holds good for a wide range of shear rates.

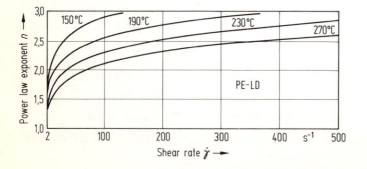

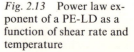

Fig. 2.13 Power law exponent of a PE-LD as a function of shear rate and temperature

Example:

The viscosity is to be calculated for a PE-LD with the following constants:

$$
\begin{aligned}
A_0 &= 4.2541 \\
A_1 &= -0.4978 \\
A_2 &= -0.0731 \\
A_3 &= 0.0133 \\
A_4 &= -0.0011 \\
b_1 &= 5.13 \cdot 10^{-6} \\
b_2 &= 5640 \text{ K}
\end{aligned}
$$

at $\dot{\gamma}_a = 500 \text{ s}^{-1}$ and $T = 200\ °C$.

Solution:

a_T from Eq. (2.3.16)

$a_T = 5.13 \cdot 10^{-6} \cdot \exp(5640/473) = 0.774$

With $X = \lg(a_T \cdot \dot{\gamma}_a)$

$X = \lg(0.774 \cdot 500) = 2.588$

η_a from Eq. (2.3.18)

$$\eta_a = 10^{(\lg a_T + A_0 + A_1 X + A_2 X^2 + A_3 X^3 + A_4 X^4)}$$

Substituting the values of A_0, A_1 and so on one gets

$\eta_a = 351.78 \text{ Pa} \cdot \text{s}$

The power law exponent is obtained from Eq. (2.3.19)

$$n = (1 + A_1 + 2A_2 X + 3A_2 X^2 + 4A_4 X^3)^{-1}$$

Using the values for A_0, A_1 and so on

$n = 3.196$

2.3.7.4   Viscosity Equation of CARREAU [11]

As shown in Fig. 2.14 [12] the Carreau equation gives the best fit for the viscosity function reproducing the asymptotic form of the plot at high and low shear rates correctly.

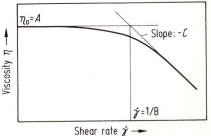

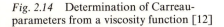

Fig. 2.14   Determination of Carreau-parameters from a viscosity function [12]

The equation is expressed as

$$\eta_a = \frac{A}{(1 + B \cdot \dot{\gamma}_a)^C} \tag{2.3.20}$$

where A, B, C are resin-dependent constants. By introducing the shift factor a_T into Eq. (2.3.20) the temperature-invariant form of the Carreau equation can be given as

$$\eta_a = \frac{A \, a_T}{(1 + B a_T \dot{\gamma}_a)^C} \tag{2.3.21}$$

For a number of resins the shift factor can be calculated as a function of temperature from the following equation with good approximation [9], [10]

$$\lg a_T(T_1, T_2) = \frac{8.86(T_1 - T_{ST})}{101.6 + (T_1 - T_{ST})} - \frac{8.86(T_2 - T_{ST})}{101.6 + (T_2 - T_{ST})} \tag{2.3.22}$$

where T_1 (°C) is the temperature, at which the viscosity is given and T_2 (°C), the temperature, at which the viscosity is to be found out.

The standard temperature T_{ST} is given by [9]

$$T_{ST} = T_g + 50 \, °C \tag{2.3.23}$$

Data on typical glass transition temperatures of polymers are given in Table 3.1 [9].

The power law exponent n can be obtained from Eq. (2.3.21):

$$\frac{1}{n} = -C \cdot \frac{B \cdot a_T}{1 + B \cdot a_T \cdot \dot{\gamma}_a} \cdot \dot{\gamma}_a + 1 \tag{2.3.24}$$

For high shear rates n becomes [12]

$$n = \frac{1}{1 - C}$$

Example:

Following constants are given for a particular PE-LD:

$$A = 32\,400 \, \text{Pa} \cdot \text{s}$$
$$B = 3.1 \, \text{s}$$
$$C = 0.62$$
$$T_{ST} = -133 \, °C$$
$$T_1 = 190 \, °C$$

The viscosity is to be calculated at

$$T_2 = 200 \, °C \quad \text{and} \quad \dot{\gamma}_a = 500 \, \text{s}^{-1}$$

Solution:

One obtains from Eq. (2.3.22)

$$X = \frac{8.86(T_1 - T_{ST})}{101.6 + (T_1 - T_{ST})} = \frac{8.86(190 - (-133))}{101.6 + (190 - (-133))} = 6.74$$

and

$$Y = \frac{8.86(T_2 - T_{ST})}{101.6 + (T_2 - T_{ST})} = \frac{8.86(200 - (-133))}{101.6 + (200 - (-133))} = 6.79$$

$$a_T = 10^{x-y} = 10^{-0.05} = 0.89$$

The power law exponent is calculated from Eq. (2.3.24)

$$n = \left(\frac{-C \cdot Z}{1+Z} + 1\right)^{-1} = \left(\frac{-0.62 \cdot 1379.5}{1 + 1379.5} + 1\right)^{-1} = 2.63$$

where $Z = B \cdot a_T \cdot \dot{\gamma}_a = 3.1 \cdot 0.89 \cdot 500 = 1379.5$

2.3.7.5 Viscosity Formula of KLEIN [14]

The regression equation of KLEIN et al. [14] is given by

$$\ln \eta_a = a_0 + a_1 \ln \dot{\gamma}_a + a_{11}(\ln \dot{\gamma}_a)^2 + a_2 T + a_{22} T^2$$
$$+ a_{12} \cdot T \cdot \ln \dot{\gamma}_a \qquad (2.3.25)$$

$T =$ Temperature of the melt ($°F$)

$\eta_a =$ Viscosity ($lb_f \cdot s/in^2$)

The resin-dependent constants a_0 to a_{22} can be determined with the help of the computer program given in [10], as has been the case in finding out the A-coefficients in Eq. (2.3.15).

Example:

Following constants are valid for a particular type of PE-LD. What is the viscosity η_a at $\dot{\gamma}_a = 500 s^{-1}$ and $T = 200°C$?

$$a_0 = \quad 3.388$$
$$a_1 = -6.351 \cdot 10^{-1}$$
$$a_{11} = -1.815 \cdot 10^{-2}$$
$$a_2 = -5.975 \cdot 10^{-3}$$
$$a_{22} = -2.51 \cdot 10^{-6}$$

and $\quad a_{12} = \quad 5.187 \cdot 10^{-4}$

Solution:

$$T(°F) = 1.8 \cdot T(°C) + 32 = 1.8 \cdot 200 + 32 = 392$$

With the constants above and Eq. (2.3.25) one gets

$$\eta_a = 0.066 \ \text{lb}_f \cdot \sec/\text{in}^2$$

and in SI-units

$$\eta_a = 6857 \cdot 0.066 = 449.8 \ \text{Pa} \cdot \text{s}$$

The expression for the power law exponent n can be derived from Eq. (2.3.13) and Eq. (2.3.25). The exponent n is given by

$$\frac{1}{n} = 1 + a_1 + 2a_{11} \ln \dot{\gamma}_a + a_{12} \cdot T \qquad (2.3.26)$$

Putting the constants $a_1 \ldots a_{12}$ into this equation one obtains

$$n = 2.919$$

2.3.7.6   Effect of Pressure on Viscosity

Compared to the influence of temperature the effect of pressure on viscosity is not of much significance.

However, the relative measure of viscosity can be obtained from [15], [16], [9]

$$\eta_p = \eta_0 \exp(\alpha_p \cdot p) \qquad (2.3.27)$$

where η_p = viscosity at pressure p and constant shear stress τ_0
η_0 = viscosity at constant shear stress τ_0
α_p = pressure coefficient

For styrene polymers η_p is calculated from [14]

$$\eta_p = \eta_0 \exp(p/1000) \qquad (2.3.28)$$

where p = pressure in bar.

Thus the change of viscosity with the pressure can be obtained from Eq. (2.3.28).

Table 2.2 shows the values of viscosity calculated according to Eq. (2.3.28) for a polystyrene of average molecular weight. It can be seen, a pressure of 200 bar causes an increase of viscosity of 22% compared to the value at 1 bar. The pressure coefficient of PE-LD is less than that of PS by a factor of 3 to 4 and the value PE-HD is again less than a factor of 2 than that of PE-LD. This means that in the case of polyethylene an increase of pressure by 200 bar would enhance the viscosity only by 3 to 4%. Consequently the effect of pressure on viscosity can be neglected in the case of extrusion processes, in which generally low pressures exist. However, in injection molding where usually one has to deal with high pressures the dependence of viscosity on pressure has to be considered.

Table 2.2   Effect of pressure on viscosity for polystyrene, Eq. (2.3.28)

$p(\text{bar})$	η_{p}
30	$1.03\,\eta_0$
100	$1.105\,\eta_0$
200	$1.221\,\eta_0$
300	$1.35\,\eta_0$
500	$1.65\,\eta_0$
1000	$2.72\,v_0$
3000	$20\,\eta_0$

2.3.7.7   Dependence of Viscosity on Molecular Weight

The relationship between viscosity and molecular weight can be described by [12]

$$\eta_{\text{a}} = K' \bar{M}_{\text{w}}^{3.5} \tag{2.3.29}$$

where M_{w} = molecular weight
  K' = resin dependent constant

The approximate value of K' for PE-LD is

  $K' = 2.28 \cdot 10^{-4}$ and for Polyamide 6

  $K' = 5.21 \cdot 10^{-14}$ according to the measurements of LAUN [21].
    These values are based on zero viscosity.

2.3.7.8   Viscosity of Two-Component Mixtures

The viscosity of a mixture consisting of the component A and the component B can be obtained from [17]

$$\lg \eta_{\text{M}} = C_{\text{A}} \lg \eta_{\text{A}} + C_{\text{B}} \lg \eta_{\text{B}} \tag{2.3.30}$$

where η = viscosity
  C = weight per cent

Indices:

M: mixture
A, B: components

2.4   Viscoelastic Behavior of Polymers

Polymer machinery can be designed sufficiently accurately on the basis of the relationships for viscous shear flow alone. However a complete analysis of melt flow should include both viscous and elastic effects, although the design of machines and dies by considering melt elasticity is rather difficult and seldom in use. All the same attempts to dimension dies taking elastic effects into account have been made as in the work of WAGNER [18] and FISCHER [19].

To give a more complete picture of melt rheology the following expressions for the viscoelastic quantities according to LAUN [20], [21] are presented. The calculation of the deformation of the bubble in film blowing is cited as an example of the application of Maxwell model.

2.4.1   Shear

2.4.1.1   Linear Viscoelastic Behavior

The linear viscoelastic behavior occurs at low shear rate or small shear.

2.4.1.1.1   Steady Shear Flow

Zero viscosity η_0 as a material function for the viscous behavior (Fig. 2.15 and Fig. 2.16):

$$\eta_0 = \frac{\tau_0}{\dot{\gamma}_0} \qquad (2.4.1)$$

Steady state shear compliance J_e^0 (Fig. 2.15 and Fig. 2.16) as a characteristic parameter for the elastic behavior:

$$J_e^0 = \frac{\gamma_{r,s}}{\tau_0} \qquad (2.4.2)$$

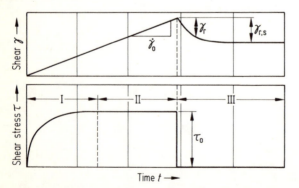

Fig. 2.15   Time dependence of shear strain and shear stress in a stressing test at constant shear rate $\dot{\gamma}_0$ and subsequent recoil due to unloading (shear stress $\tau = 0$) with $\gamma_{r,s}$ as recoverable shear strain [21]

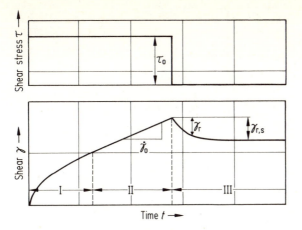

Fig. 2.16 Creep test at constant shear stress τ_0 and subsequent retardation after unloading (shear stress $\tau = 0$) [20]. $\gamma_{r,s}$ = recoverable shear strain; I = initial state; II = steady state; III = retardation

2.4.1.1.2 Time-dependent Behavior

Viscosity $\mathring{\eta}(t)$ (Fig. 2.17):

$$\mathring{\eta}(t) = \frac{\tau(t)}{\dot{\gamma}_0} \tag{2.4.3}$$

Shear compliance $\mathring{J}(t)$ (Fig. 2.18):

$$\mathring{J}(t) = \frac{\gamma(t)}{\tau_0} \tag{2.4.4}$$

Maximum time of retardation τ_{max} as a rheological quantity for the transient behavior (Fig. 2.19):

$$\gamma_r(t) \approx \gamma_{r,s}[1 - \exp(-t/\tau_{max})] \tag{2.4.5}$$

Shear stress relaxation modulus $\mathring{G}(t)$ (Fig. 2.20 and Fig. 2.21):

$$\mathring{G}(t) = \frac{\tau(t)}{\gamma_0} \tag{2.4.6}$$

Dependance of storage modulus G' and loss modulus G'' on frequency (Fig. 2.22) with sinusoidal shear strain γ:

$$\gamma = \hat{\gamma} \sin \omega t \tag{2.4.7}$$

Sinusoidal and out of phase shear stress τ:

$$\tau = \hat{\gamma}(G' \sin \omega t + G'' \cos \omega t) \tag{2.4.8}$$

where $\hat{\gamma}$ = amplitude of shear
ω = angular frequency

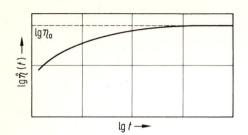

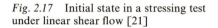

Fig. 2.17   Initial state in a stressing test under linear shear flow [21]

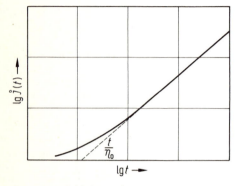

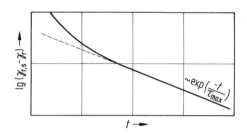

Fig. 2.18   Initial state in creep under linear shear flow [21]

Fig. 2.19   Retardation from steady shear flow [21] (shear stress $\tau = 0$ at time $t = 0$)

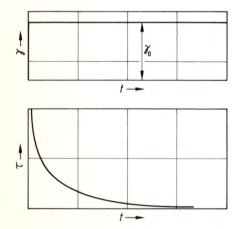

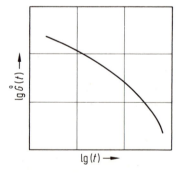

Fig. 2.21   Relaxation modulus of linear shear flow [21]

Fig. 2.20   Relaxation after a step shear strain γ_0 [21]

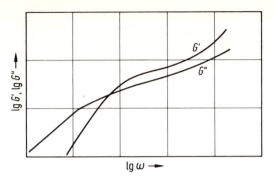

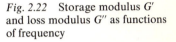

Fig. 2.22 Storage modulus G' and loss modulus G'' as functions of frequency

The storage modulus $G'(\omega)$ characterizes the elastic behavior, whereas the loss modulus G'' depicts the viscous behavior of the melt subjected to periodic shear deformation:

Expressions for conversion:

Determination of zero viscosity and shear compliance from relaxation modulus [21]:

$$\eta_0 = \int\limits_0^t \mathring{G}(t)\,\mathrm{d}t \tag{2.4.9}$$

$$J_e^0 = \frac{1}{\eta_0^2} \int\limits_0^\infty t\mathring{G}(t)\,\mathrm{d}t \tag{2.4.10}$$

Determination of zero viscosity and shear compliance from storage and loss moduli [21]:

$$\eta_0 = \lim_{\omega \to 0} \frac{G''}{\omega} \tag{2.4.11}$$

$$J_e^0 = \frac{1}{\eta_0^2} \lim_{\omega \to 0} \frac{G'}{\omega^2} \tag{2.4.12}$$

2.4.1.2 Nonlinear Viscoelastic Behavior

2.4.1.2.1 Steady Shear Flow

The viscosity

$$\eta = \frac{\tau_0}{\dot{\gamma}_0}$$

and the shear compliance

$$J_e = \frac{\gamma_{r,s}}{\tau_0}$$

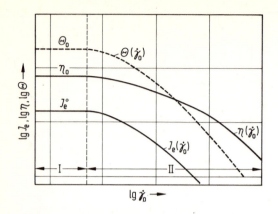

Fig. 2.23 Parameters for steady shear flow [21].
I = linear region; II = nonlinear region

are dependent on the shear rate and shear stress respectively in the nonlinear case. Their limiting values for small shear rates or shear stresses are η_0 and J_e^0 (Fig. 2.23). Another material function in addition to the shear compliance characterizing the elastic behavior is the primary normal stress coefficient Θ with N_1 as the normal stress difference:

$$\Theta = \frac{N_1}{\dot{\gamma}_0^2} \tag{2.4.13}$$

The limiting value of the normal stress function $\Theta(\dot{\gamma}_0)$ (Fig. 2.23) at small shear rates is given by

$$\Theta_0 = \lim_{\dot{\gamma}_0 \to 0} \Theta(\dot{\gamma}_0) \tag{2.4.14}$$

Further we have:

$$J_e = \frac{\Theta}{2\eta^2} \tag{2.4.15}$$

2.4.1.2.2 Characterization of the Transient State

Initial state in a stressing test (Fig. 2.24)

$$\eta(t) \leqq \mathring{\eta}(t) \tag{2.4.16}$$

$\mathring{\eta}(t)$ is the asymptote.

Plots of starting state in creep test (Fig. 2.25)

$$J(t) \geqq \mathring{J}(t) \tag{2.4.17}$$

$\mathring{J}(t)$ is asymptote.

Relaxation modul (Fig. 2.26):

$$G(t) = h(\gamma_0)\,\mathring{G}(t) \tag{2.4.18}$$

The time-dependent behavior remains unchanged in the nonlinear case. The whole function plot will be displaced by the factor $h(\gamma_0)$.

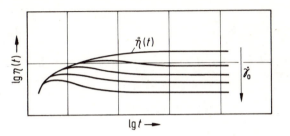

Fig. 2.24   Initial state in a stressing test of nonlinear shear flow [21]

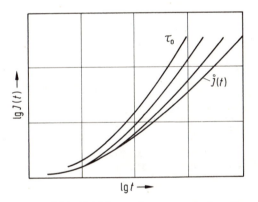

Fig. 2.25   Initial state in creep test of nonlinear shear flow [21]

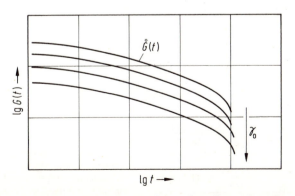

Fig. 2.26   Relaxation modulus of nonlinear shear flow [21]

2.4.2   Uniaxial Tension

2.4.2.1   Linear Viscoelastic Behavior

2.4.2.1.1   Steady Tensile Extensional Flow

Tensile zero viscosity μ_0 as a material function for the viscous behavior (Fig. 2.27 and Fig. 2.28)

$$\mu_0 = \frac{\sigma_0}{\dot{\varepsilon}_0} \tag{2.4.19}$$

Steady state tensile compliance D_e^0 as material function for the elastic behavior:

$$D_e^0 = \frac{\varepsilon_{r,s}}{\sigma_0} \tag{2.4.20}$$

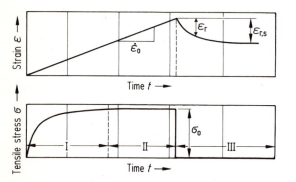

Fig. 2.27   Time dependence of tensile strain and tensile stress at constant tensile strain rate $\dot{\varepsilon}_0$ and subsequent retardation after unloading (tensile stress $\tau = 0$) [2]. $\varepsilon_{r,s}$ = recoverable tensile strain; I = initial state; II = steady state; III = retardation

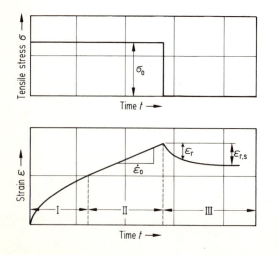

Fig. 2.28   Tensile creep at constant tensile stress τ_0 and subsequent retardation after unloading (tensile stress $\tau = 0$) [21]

2.4.2.1.2   Transient Behavior

Tensile viscosity $\mathring{\mu}(t)$ (Fig. 2.29)

$$\mathring{\mu}(t) = \frac{\sigma(t)}{\dot{\varepsilon}_0} \tag{2.4.21}$$

$$\mathring{\mu}(t) = 3\,\mathring{\eta}(t) \tag{2.4.22}$$

$$\mu_0 = 3\,\eta_0$$

The tensile viscosity is three times the shear viscosity.

Tensile creep compliance $\mathring{D}(t)$ (Fig. 2.30):

$$\mathring{D}(t) = \frac{\varepsilon(t)}{\sigma_0} \tag{2.4.23}$$

$$\mathring{D}(t) = \frac{1}{3} \cdot \mathring{J}(t) \tag{2.4.24}$$

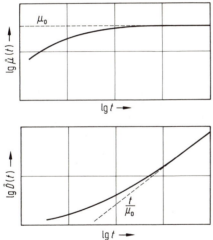

Fig. 2.29   Initial state of linear tensile extension [21]

Fig. 2.30   Initial state in tensile creep under linear tensile extension [21]

Maximum retardation time τ_{max} (Fig. 2.31)

$$\varepsilon_r(t) \approx \varepsilon_{r,s}[1 - \exp(-t/\tau_{max})] \tag{2.4.25}$$

Relaxation after a step strain of ε_0:

Tensile relaxation modulus $\mathring{E}(t)$ (Fig. 2.32):

$$\mathring{E}(t) = \frac{\sigma(t)}{\varepsilon_0} \tag{2.4.26}$$

$$\mathring{E}(t) = 3 \cdot \mathring{G}(t) \tag{2.4.27}$$

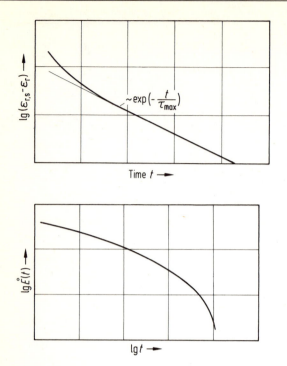

Fig. 2.31   Retardation from steady-state tensile extension [21]

Fig. 2.32   Tensile relaxation modulus of tensile extensional flow [21]

2.4.2.2   Nonlinear Viscoelastic Behavior

2.4.2.2.1   Steady Tensile Extensional Flow

As shown in Fig. 2.5, the tensile viscosity μ is given by

$$\mu = \frac{\sigma_0}{\dot{\varepsilon}_0}$$

Tensile compliance D_e (Fig. 2.33)

$$D_e = \frac{\varepsilon_{r,s}}{\sigma_0}$$

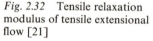

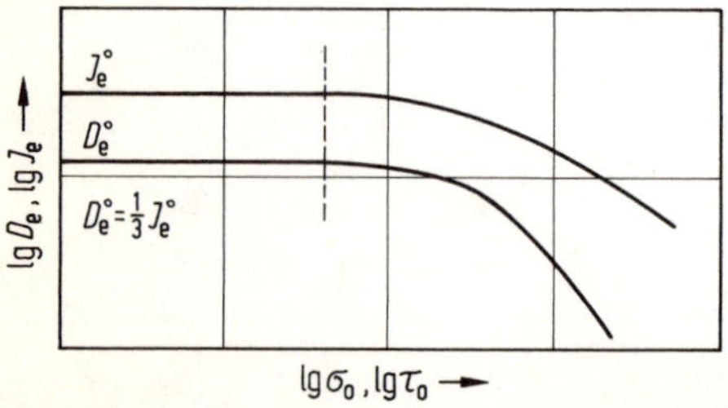

Fig. 2.33   Plot of tensile compliance D_e and shear compliance J_e [21]

2.4.2.2.2 Time-dependent Behavior

Plots of starting state in tension test (Fig. 2.34) [21]

$$\mu(t) \geqq \mathring{\mu}(t) \tag{2.4.28}$$

$\mathring{\mu}(t)$ is an asymptote.

Start-up curves in a tensile creep test (Fig. 2.35) [21]

$$D(t) \leqq \mathring{D}(t) \tag{2.4.29}$$

$\mathring{D}(t)$ is an asymptote.

Tensile relaxation modulus (Fig. 2.36)

$$E(t, \varepsilon_0) = g(\varepsilon_0) \cdot \mathring{E}(t) \tag{2.4.30}$$

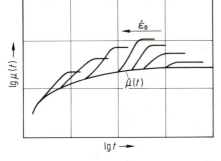

Fig. 2.34   Initial state of nonlinear tensile extension [21]

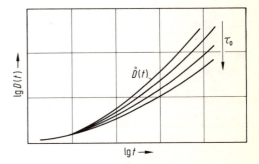

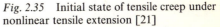

Fig. 2.35   Initial state of tensile creep under nonlinear tensile extension [21]

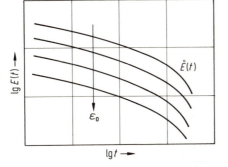

Fig. 2.36   Tensile relaxation modulus as a function of time under nonlinear tensile extension [21]

2.4.3   Maxwell Model

The viscoelastic properties of a polymer can be used to calculate the deformation of a bubble in a film blowing process. In such a case, due to its simplicity the Maxwell model, which consists of a body defined as an ideal spring and dashpot in series (Fig. 2.37) can be applied [18], [19].

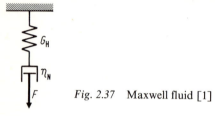

Fig. 2.37   Maxwell fluid [1]

The total rate of deformation $\dot{\gamma}$ is the sum of the elastic component $\dot{\gamma}_H$ and viscous component $\dot{\gamma}_N$

$$\dot{\gamma} = \dot{\gamma}_H + \dot{\gamma}_N \tag{2.4.31}$$

leading to [22]

$$\eta_N \dot{\gamma} = t_s \dot{\tau} + \tau \tag{2.4.32}$$

where

$$t_s = \frac{\eta_N}{G_H} \tag{2.4.33}$$

The time t_s is called the relaxation time, as the stress τ relaxes with the time.

η_N = newtonian viscosity
G_H = elastic shear modulus of the spring (Hooke element)

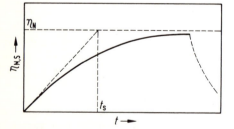

Fig. 2.38   Tensile viscosity of Maxwell fluid [1]

At a given rate of deformation the viscosity $\eta_{N,s}$ reaches asymptotically the Newtonian value (Fig. 2.38). After the release of strain the stress delays according to

$$\tau = \tau_0 \exp(-t/t_s) \tag{2.4.34}$$

It can be seen from Eq. (2.4.34) that the relaxation time is the period, in which the stress fall to $1/e$ (37 per cent) of its original value [23]. It also follows from

Eq. (2.4.34) that the modulus of relaxation for $\gamma = \gamma_0$, G is given by

$$G = G_0 \exp(-t/t_s) \tag{2.4.35}$$

The expression for the elongation of the bubble is a film blowing process can now be given as

$$\sigma + t_s \frac{\partial \sigma}{\partial t} = \mu \frac{dv}{dx} \tag{2.4.36}$$

where σ = tensile stress,
  t_s = relaxation time
  μ = tensile viscosity of the melt
  v = vertical velocity component of the bubble,
  x = axial coordinate

As the elongation of the bubble occurs biaxially, the deformation in the circumferential direction has to be calculated on similar lines. If it is assumed that the tensile viscosities and the relaxation times in both directions are equal, the influence of viscoelasticity on the bubble form can be predicted [18]. WAGNER [18] estimates the relaxation time in the order of 5 to 11 seconds depending on the operating conditions.

2.4.4   Practical Formulas for Die Swell and Extensional Flow

Elastics effects are responsible for die swell, which occurs when the melt flows through a die as shown in Fig. 2.39 [20].

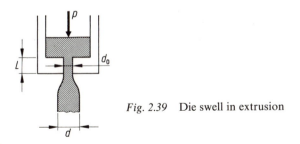

Fig. 2.39   Die swell in extrusion

The following equation is given by COGSWELL [24] for the die swell:

$$B_L^2 = \frac{2}{3} \gamma_R \left[\left(1 + \frac{1}{\gamma_R^2} \right)^{\frac{3}{2}} - \frac{1}{\gamma_R^3} \right] \tag{2.4.37}$$

where B_L = die swell $\dfrac{d}{d_0}$ (Fig. 2.39) in a capillary of length to diameter ratio greater than 16
  γ_R = recoverable shear strain

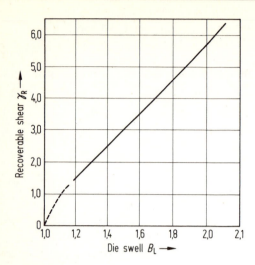

Fig. 2.40   Dependence of recoverable shear on die swell [24]

In Fig. 2.40 the recoverable shear strain is presented as a function of die swell according to Eq. (2.4.37) [24].

2.4.4.2   Extensional Flow

Following relationships for extensional flow of melt after COGSWELL [24] are of importance for the practice:

Elongational stress τ_E:

$$\sigma_E = \frac{3}{8}(n_R + 1) \cdot p_c \tag{2.4.38}$$

Tensile viscosity μ:

$$\mu = \frac{9}{32} \cdot \frac{(n_R + 1)^2}{\eta_a} \cdot \left(\frac{p_c}{\dot{\gamma}_a}\right)^2 \tag{2.4.39}$$

Reversible extension ε_R:

$$\varepsilon_R = \ln B_0^2 \tag{2.4.40}$$

Rupture stress σ_R:

$$\sigma_R = \frac{3}{8}(3n_R + 1) \cdot p_c \tag{2.4.41}$$

where n_R = reciprocal of power lax index n in Eq. (2.3.10)
        p_c = entrance pressure loss according to Eq. (2.3.2)
  $\dot{\gamma}_a, \eta_a$ = apparent shear rate and apparent shear viscosity, respectively
        B_0 = die swell in melt flow through an orifice with zero length

Literature

[1] PAHL, M., BALDUHN, R., LINNEMANN, D.: Praktische Rheologie der Kunststoffschmelzen und Lösungen, VDI-Kunststofftechnik, Düsseldorf (1982)
[2] MÜNSTEDT, H.: Kunststoffe 68, 92 (1978)
[3] Kunststoff-Physik im Gespräch, brochure, BASF, 1977
[4] EYRING, H.: I. Chem. Phys. 4, 283 (1963)
[5] PRANDTL, L.: Phys. Blätter 5, 161 (1949)
[6] OSTWALD, W.: Kolloid-Z., 36, 99 (1925)
[7] DE WAALE, A.: Oil and Color Chem. Assoc. J., 6, 33 (1923)
[8] RAO, N.S.: Berechnen von Extrudierwerkzeugen, VDI-Verlag, Düsseldorf (1978)
[9] RAUWENDAAL, C.: Polymer Extrusion, Hanser, Munich (1986)
[10] RAO, N.S.: Designing Machines and Dies for Polymer Processing with Computer Programs, Hanser, Munich (1981)
[11] CARREAU, P.J.: Dissertation, Univ. Wisconsin, Madison (1968)
[12] HERTLEIN, T., FRITZ, H.G.: Kunststoffe 78, 606 (1988)
[13] MICHAELI, W.: Extrusion Dies, Hanser, Munich (1984)
[14] KLEIN, I., MARSHALL, D.I., FRIEHE, C.A.: Soc. Plastics Engrs. J. 21, 1299 (1965)
[15] AVENAS, P., AGASSANT, J.F., SERGENT, J.PH.: La Mise en Forme des Matières Plastiques, Technique & Documentation (Lavoisier), Paris (1982)
[16] MÜNSTEDT, H.: Berechnen von Extrudierwerkzeugen, VDI-Verlag, Düsseldorf (1978)
[17] CARLEY, J.F.: Antec 84, S. 439
[18] WAGNER, M.H.: Dissertation, Univ. Stuttgart (1976)
[19] FISCHER, E.: Dissertation, Univ. Stuttgart (1983)
[20] LAUN, H.M.: Rheol. Acta 18, 478 (1979)
[21] LAUN, H.M.: Progr. Colloid & Polymer Sci. 75, 111 (1987)
[22] BRYDSON, J.A.: Flow Properties of Polymer Melts, Iliffe Books, London (1970)
[23] BERNHARDT, E.C.: Processing of Thermoplastic Materials, Reinhold, New York (1963)
[24] COGSWELL, F.N.: Polymer Melt Rheology, John Wiley, New York (1981)

3 Thermodynamic Properties of Polymers

In addition to the rheological data, thermodynamic properties of polymers are necessary for designing machines and dies. It is often the case in design work that the local values of these data are required as functions of temperature and pressure. Besides physical relationships, this chapter presents regression equations developed from experimental data for calculating thermodynamic properties, as these polynomials are often used in the practice as in the case of data acquisition for data banks [1].

3.1 Specific Volume

According to the Spencer-Gilmore equation which is similar to the Van-der-Waal equation of state for real gases the relationship between pressure p, specific volume v and temperature T of a polymer can be written as

$$(v - b^*)(p + p^*) = \frac{RT}{W} \tag{3.1.1}$$

In this equation b^* is the specific individual volume of the macromolecule, p^*, the cohesion pressure, W, the molecular weight of the monomer and R, the universal gas constant [2].

Example:

Following values are given for a PE-LD:

$W = 28.1$ g/Mol;
$b^* = 0.875$ cm^3/g
$p^* = 3240$ atm

Calculate the specific volume v at

$T = 190$ °C and $p = 1$ bar.

Solution:

Using Eq. (3.1.1) and the conversion factors to obtain the volume v in cm^3/g, we obtain

$$v = \frac{10 \times 8.314 \times (273 + 190)}{28.1 \times 3240.99 \times 1.013} + 0.875 = 1.292 \text{ cm}^3/\text{g}$$

The density ϱ is the reciprocal value of the specific volume so that

$$\varrho = \frac{1}{v} \tag{3.1.2}$$

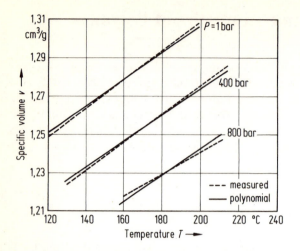

Fig. 3.1   Specific volume as a function of temperature and pressure for PE-LD [1]

The functional relationship between specific volume v, pressure p and temperature T can also be fitted by a polynomial of the form [1], [3]

$$v = A(0)_v + A(1)_v \cdot p + A(2)_v \cdot T + A(3)_v \cdot T \cdot p \tag{3.1.3}$$

if experimental data is available (Fig. 3.1). The empirical coefficients $A(0)_v$ ... $A(1)_v$ can be determined by means of the computer program given in [1].

3.2   Specific Heat

The specific heat c_p is defined as

$$c_p = \left(\frac{\partial h}{\partial T}\right)_p \tag{3.2.1}$$

where h = Enthalpy
       T = Temperature

The specific heat c_p gives the amount of heat, which is supplied to a system in a reversible process at a constant pressure in order to increase the temperature of the substance by dT.

The specific heat at constant volume c_v is given by

$$c_v = \left(\frac{\partial u}{\partial T}\right)_v \tag{3.2.2}$$

where u = internal energy
       T = temperature

In the case of c_v the supply of heat to the system occurs at constant volume.

c_p and c_v are related to each other through the Spencer-Gilmore equation Eq. (3.1.1):

$$c_v = c_p - \frac{R}{W}$$

(3.2.3)

The numerical values of c_p and c_v differ by roughly 10%, so that for approximate calculations c_v can be made equal to c_p [2].

Plots of c_p as function of temperature are shown in Fig. 3.2 for amorphous, semi-crystalline and crystalline polymers.

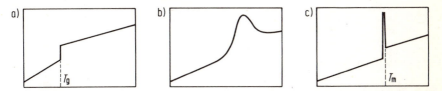

Fig. 3.2   Specific heat as a function of temperature for amorphous (a), semi-crystalline (b) and crystalline polymers (c) [4]

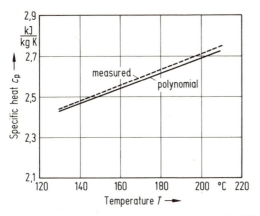

Fig. 3.3   Comparison between measured values of c_p [6] and polynomial for PE-LD [1]

As shown in Fig. 3.3 the measured values can be fitted by a polynomial of the type

$$c_p(T) = A(0)\, c_p + A(1)\, c_p \cdot T + A(2)\, c_p \cdot T^2$$

(3.2.4)

The use of thermal properties c_p and ϱ in design problems is illustrated in the examples given in Chapter 6.

The expansion coefficient α_v at constant pressure is given by [4]

$$\alpha_v = \frac{1}{v} \left(\frac{\partial v}{\partial T} \right)_p$$

(3.2.5)

The linear expansion coefficient α_{lin} is approximately

$$\alpha_{lin} \approx \frac{1}{3}\alpha_v \qquad (3.2.6)$$

The isothermal compression coefficient γ_K is defined as [4]

$$\gamma_K = -\frac{1}{v}\left(\frac{\partial v}{\partial p}\right)_T \qquad (3.2.7)$$

α_v and γ_K are related to each other by the expression [4]

$$c_p = c_v + \frac{T \cdot v \cdot \alpha_v^2}{\gamma_K} \qquad (3.2.8)$$

3.3 Enthalpy

Eq. (3.2.1) leads to

$$dh = c_p \cdot dT \qquad (3.3.1)$$

As shown in Fig. 3.4 the measured data on $h = h(T)$ [6] for a polymer melt can be fitted by the polynomial

$$h(T) = A(0)_h + A(1)_h \cdot T + A(2)_h \cdot T^2 \qquad (3.3.2)$$

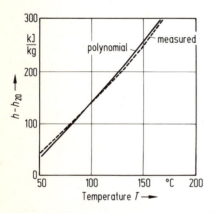

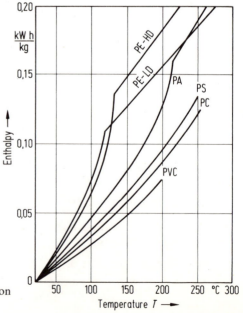

Fig. 3.4 Comparison between measured values of h [6] and polynomial for PA-6 [1]

Fig. 3.5 Specific enthalpy as a function of temperature [4]

The specific enthalpy defined as the total energy supplied to the polymer divided by throughput of the polymer is a useful parameter for designing extrusion and injection molding equipment such as screws. It gives the theoretical amount of energy required to bring the solid polymer to the process temperature.

Values of this parameter for different polymers are given in Fig. 3.5 [4].

If, for example, the throughput of an extruder is 100 kg/h of polyamide (PA) and the processing temperature is 260 °C, the theoretical power requirement would be 20 kW. This can be assumed to be a safe design value for the motor horse power, although theoretically it includes the power supply to the polymer by the heater bands of the extruder as well.

3.4 Thermal Conductivity

The thermal conductivity λ is defined as

$$\lambda = \frac{Q \cdot l}{t \cdot A \cdot (T_1 - T_2)} \tag{3.4.1}$$

where Q = heat flow through the surface of area A in a period of time t

$(T_1 - T_2)$ = temperature difference over the length l

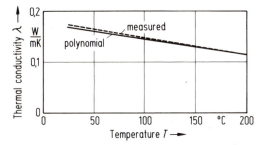

Fig. 3.6 Comparison between measured values of λ [6] and polynomial for PP [1]

Analogous to the specific heat c_p and enthalpy h the thermal conductivity λ as shown in Fig. 3.6 can be expressed as [1]

$$\lambda(T) = A(0)_\lambda + A(1)_\lambda \cdot T + A(2)_\lambda \cdot T^2 \tag{3.4.2}$$

The thermal conductivity increases only slightly with the pressure. A pressure increase from 1 bar to 250 bar leads only to an increase of less than 5% of its value at 1 bar.

Within a particular resin category like PE-LD, PE-HD and so on the thermal properties are largely independent of the molecular structure. Exhaustive measured data of the quantities c_p, h and λ and pressure-volume-temperature diagrams of polymers are given in the VDMA-Handbook [5].

Approximate values of thermal properties which are of use to plastics engineers are summarised in Table 3.1 [4].

Table 3.1   Approximate values for the thermal properties of some polymers [4]

Polymer	Thermal conductivity	Specific heat	Density	Glass transition temperature	Melting point range
	$\lambda\,[\mathrm{W/m\cdot K}]$	$c_p\,[\mathrm{kJ/kg\,K}]$	$\varrho\,[\mathrm{g/cm^3}]$	$T_g\,[°\mathrm{C}]$	$T_m\,[°\mathrm{C}]$
PS	0.12	1.20	1.06	101	–
PVC	0.21	1.10	1.40	80	–
PMMA	0.20	1.45	1.18	105	–
SAN	0.12	1.40	1.08	115	–
ABS	0.25	1.40	1.02	115	–
PC	0.19	1.40	1.20	150	–
PE-LD	0.24	2.30	0.92	– 120/–90	ca. 110
PE-LLD	0.24	2.30	0.92	– 120/–90	ca. 125
PE-HD	0.25	2.25	0.95	– 120/–90	ca. 130
PP	0.15	2.10	0.91	– 10	160–170
PA-6	0.25	2.15	1.13	50	215–225
PA-6.6	0.24	2.15	1.14	55	250–260
PET	0.29	1.55	1.35	70	250–260
PBT	0.21	1.25	1.35	45	ca. 220

Literature

[1] RAO, N.S.: Designing Machines and Dies for Polymer Processing, Hanser, Munich (1981)
[2] KALIVODA, P.: Lecture, Seminar: Optimieren von Kunststoffmaschinen und -werkzeugen mit EDV, Haus der Technik, Essen (1982)
[3] MÜNSTEDT, H.: Berechnen von Extrudierwerkzeugen, VDI-Verlag, Düsseldorf (1978)
[4] RAUWENDAAL, C.: Polymer Extrusion, Hanser, Munich (1986)
[5] Kenndaten für die Verarbeitung thermoplastischer Kunststoffe, Teil I, Thermodynamik, Hanser, München (1979)
[6] Proceedings, 9. Kunststofftechnisches Kolloquium, IKV, Aachen (1978) p. 52

4   Formulas of Heat Transfer

Heat transfer and flow processes occur in most of the polymer processing machinery and often determine the production rate. Designing and optimizing machine elements and processes therefore requires the knowledge of the fundamentsls of these sciences. The flow behavior of polymer melts has been dealt with in Chapter 2. In the present chapter the principles of heat transfer of relevance to polymer processing are treated with examples.

4.1   Steady-state Conduction

The Fourier's law for one dimensional conduction is given by

$$\dot{Q} = -\lambda A \frac{dT}{dx} \tag{4.1.1}$$

where $\dot{Q}$ = heat flow
λ = thermal conductivity
A = area perpendicular to the direction of heat flow
T = temperature
x = distance (Fig. 4.1)

Fig. 4.1   Plane wall [1]

4.1.1   Plane Wall

Temperatur profile (Fig. 4.1) [1]:

$$T(x) = \frac{(T_{w_2} - T_{w_1})}{\delta} \cdot x + T_{w_1} \tag{4.1.2}$$

Heat flow:

$$\dot{Q} = \frac{\lambda}{\delta} \cdot A \cdot (T_{w_1} - T_{w_2}) \tag{4.1.3}$$

Analogous to Ohm's law in electric-circuit theory Eq. (4.1.3) can be written as [2]

$$\dot{Q} = \frac{\Delta T}{R} \tag{4.1.4}$$

in which

$$R = \frac{\delta}{\lambda \cdot A}$$ (4.1.5)

where ΔT = temperature difference
         δ = wall thickness
         R = thermal resistance

Example:

The temperatures of a plastic sheet 30 mm thick with a thermal conductivity λ = 0.335 W/(m.K) are according to Fig. 4.1 T_{w_1} = 100 °C and T_{w_2} = 40 °C. Calculate the heat flow per unit area of the sheet.

Solution:

Substituting the given values in Eq. (4.1.3) we obtain

$$\frac{\dot{Q}}{A} = \frac{0.335}{(30/1000)} \cdot (100 - 40) = 670 \frac{W}{m^2}$$

4.1.2   Cylinder (Fig. 4.2) [1]

Temperature distribution:

$$T(r) = T_{w_1} + \frac{(T_{w_2} - T_{w_1})}{\ln\left(\frac{r_2}{r_1}\right)} \cdot \ln\left(\frac{r}{r_1}\right)$$ (4.1.6)

Heat flow:

$$\dot{Q} = \frac{\lambda}{\delta} \cdot A_m (T_{w_1} - T_{w_2})$$ (4.1.7)

with the log. mean surface area A_m of the cylinder

$$A_m = \frac{A_2 - A_1}{\ln\left(\frac{A_2}{A_1}\right)}$$ (4.1.8)

where $\delta = r_2 - r_1$.

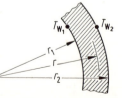

Fig. 4.2   Cylindrical wall [1]

4.1.3 Hollow Sphere

Temperature distribution [1]:

$$T(r) = \frac{1}{r} \frac{(T_{w_1} - T_{w_2}) r_1 r_2}{(r_2 - r_1)} - \frac{(T_{w_1 r_1} - T_{w_2 r_2})}{(r_2 - r_1)} \tag{4.1.9}$$

with the boundary conditions

$$T(r = r_1) = T_{w_1} \quad \text{and} \quad T(r = r_2) = T_{w_2}$$

Heat flow:

$$\dot{Q} = \frac{\lambda}{\delta} \cdot A_m \cdot (T_{w_1} - T_{w_2}) \tag{4.1.10}$$

The geometrical mean area A_m of the sphere is

$$A_m = \sqrt{A_1 A_2} \tag{4.1.11}$$

The wall thickness δ is

$$\delta = r_2 - r_1 \tag{4.1.12}$$

4.1.4 Sphere

Heat flow from a sphere in an infinite medium ($r_2 \to \infty$) [1]

$$\dot{Q} = 4 \pi r_1 \lambda (T_{w_1} - T_\infty) \tag{4.1.13}$$

where T_∞ = temperature at a very large distance.

Fig. 4.3 shows the temperature profiles of the one-dimensional bodies treated above [1].

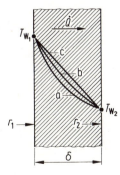

Fig. 4.3   One-dimensional heat transfer [1]
a: sphere, b: cylinder, c: plate

4.1.5   Heat Conduction in Composite Walls

Following the electrical analogy heat conduction through a multiple-layer wall can be treated as a current flowing through resistances connected in series. From this concept we obtain for the heat flow through the composite wall shown in Fig. 4.4

$$T_{w_1} - T_{w_2} = \dot{Q}\,\frac{\delta_1}{\lambda_1\,A_1} \tag{4.1.14}$$

$$T_{w_2} - T_{w_3} = \frac{\dot{Q}\,\delta_2}{\lambda_2\,A_2} \tag{4.1.15}$$

$$T_{w_3} - T_{w_4} = \frac{\dot{Q}\,\delta_3}{\lambda_3\,A_3} \tag{4.1.16}$$

Adding Eqns. (4.1.14) to (4.1.16) and putting $A_1 = A_2 = A_3 = A$ gives

$$T_{w_1} - T_{w_4} = \frac{\dot{Q}\,\delta_1}{\lambda_1\,A} + \frac{\dot{Q}\,\delta_2}{\lambda_2\,A} + \frac{\dot{Q}\,\delta_3}{\lambda_3\,A} = \Delta T \tag{4.1.17}$$

Thus

$$\dot{Q} = \frac{\Delta T}{\left(\dfrac{\delta_1}{\lambda_1\,A} + \dfrac{\delta_2}{\lambda_2\,A} + \dfrac{\delta_3}{\lambda_3\,A}\right)} \tag{4.1.18}$$

Inserting the conduction resistances

$$R_1 = \frac{\delta_1}{\lambda_1\,A_1} \tag{4.1.19}$$

$$R_2 = \frac{\delta_2}{\lambda_2\,A_2} \tag{4.1.20}$$

$$R_3 = \frac{\delta_3}{\lambda_3\,A_3} \tag{4.1.21}$$

into Eq. (4.1.18) we get

$$\dot{Q} = \frac{\Delta T}{(R_1 + R_2 + R_3)} = \frac{\Delta T}{R} \tag{4.1.22}$$

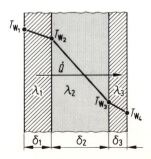

Fig. 4.4   Heat transfer through a composite wall [1]

Example 1:

A two-layer wall consists of following insulating materials (see Fig. 4.4):

$$\delta_1 = 16 \text{ mm}, \qquad \lambda_1 = 0.048 \frac{W}{m \cdot K}$$

$$\delta_2 = 140 \text{ mm}, \qquad \lambda_2 = 0.033 \frac{W}{m \cdot K}$$

The temperatures are $T_{w_1} = 30 \text{ °C}$; $T_{w_2} = 2 \text{ °C}$.

Calculate the heat loss per unit area of the wall.

Solution:

$$\Delta T = T_{w_1} - T_{w_2} = 30 - 2 = 28 \text{ °C}$$

Area $A = 1 \text{ m}^2$

$$R_1 = \frac{\delta_1}{\lambda_1 A} = \frac{(16/1000)}{0.048 * 1} = 0.33 \frac{K}{W}$$

$$R_2 = \frac{\delta_2}{\lambda_2 A} = \frac{(140/1000)}{0.033 * 1} = 4.24 \frac{K}{W}$$

$$\dot{Q} = \frac{\Delta T}{(R_1 + R_2)} = \frac{28}{(4.24 + 0.33)} = 6.13 \text{ W}$$

The following example [2] illustrates the calculation of heat transfer through a tube shown in Fig. 4.5.

Example 2:

A tube with an outside diameter of 60 mm is insulated with following materials:

$$\delta_1 = 50 \text{ mm}, \qquad \lambda_1 = 0.055 \text{ W/(m} \cdot \text{K)}$$
$$\delta_2 = 40 \text{ mm}, \qquad \lambda_2 = 0.05 \quad \text{W/(m} \cdot \text{K)}.$$

The temperatures are $T_{w_1} = 150 \text{ °C}$ and $T_{w_2} = 30 \text{ °C}$. Calculate the heat loss per unit length of the tube.

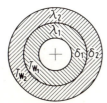

Fig. 4.5   Heat flow in a multilayered cylinder

Solution:

Resistance R_1:

$$R_1 = \frac{\delta_1}{\lambda \bar{A}_1} = \frac{0.05}{0.055 * 2\pi \bar{r}_1 \cdot L} \frac{K}{W}$$

average radius $\bar{r}_1$:

$$\bar{r}_1 = \frac{(80-30)}{\ln\left(\frac{80}{30}\right)} = 50.97 \text{ mm}$$

$$R_1 = \frac{2.839}{L} \frac{K}{W}$$

Resistance R_2:

$$R_2 = \frac{\delta_2}{\lambda_2 \bar{A}_2} = \frac{0.04}{0.05 * 2\pi \bar{r}_2 L} \frac{K}{W}$$

average radius $\bar{r}_2$:

$$\bar{r}_2 = \frac{(120-80)}{\ln\left(\frac{120}{80}\right)} = 98.64 \text{ mm}$$

$$R_2 = \frac{1.291}{L} \frac{K}{W}$$

Heat loss per unit length of the tube according to Eq. (4.1.22):

$$\frac{\dot{Q}}{L} = \frac{(150-30)}{(2.839+1.291)} = 29.1 \text{ W/m.}$$

In the case of multiple-layer walls, in which the heat flow is divided into parallel flows as shown in Fig. 4.6 the total heat flow is the sum of the individual heat flows. Therefore we have

$$\dot{Q} = \sum_{i=1}^{z} \dot{Q}_i \tag{4.1.23}$$

$$\dot{Q} = \sum_{i=1}^{z} (\lambda_i A_i) \frac{(T_{w_1} - T_{w_2})}{\delta} \tag{4.1.24}$$

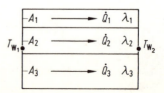

Fig. 4.6 Heat transfer in composite walls in parallel [1]

4.1.6 Overall Heat Transfer through Composite Walls

If heat exchange takes place between a fluid and a wall as shown in Fig. 4.6a then we have in addition to the conduction resistance convection resistance also, which can be written as

$$R_{\ddot{u}_1} = \frac{1}{\alpha_1 A_1} \tag{4.1.25}$$

where α_i = heat-transfer coefficient in the boundary layer near the walls adjacent to the fluids.

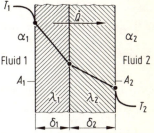

Fig. 4.6a Conduction and convection through a composite wall [1]

The combination of convection and conduction in stationary walls is called overall heat transfer and can be expressed as

$$\dot{Q} = kA(T_1 - T_2) = \frac{1}{R_w}(T_1 - T_2) \tag{4.1.26}$$

where k is denoted as the overall heat-transfer coefficient with the corresponding overall resistance R_w

$$R_w = \frac{1}{kA} \tag{4.1.27}$$

Analogous to conduction for the composite wall in Fig. 4.6a the overall resistance R_w can be given by

$$R_w = R_{\ddot{u}_1} + \sum_{i=1}^{z} R_i + R_{\ddot{u}_2} \tag{4.1.28}$$

or

$$\frac{1}{kA} = \frac{1}{\alpha_1 A_1} + \sum_{i=1}^{z} \frac{\delta_i}{\lambda_i A_i} + \frac{1}{\alpha_2 A_2} \tag{4.1.29}$$

A simplified form of Eq. (4.1.29) is

$$k = \frac{1}{\dfrac{1}{\alpha_1} + \displaystyle\sum_{i=1}^{z} \dfrac{\delta_i}{\lambda_i} + \dfrac{1}{\alpha_2}} \tag{4.1.30}$$

Calculation of the convection heat-transfer coefficient is shown in the Section 4.5.

4.2   Unsteady-state Conduction

The differential equation for the transient one-dimensional conduction after Fourier is given by

$$\frac{\partial T}{\partial t} = a \frac{\partial^2 T}{\partial x^2} \tag{4.2.1}$$

where T = temperature
      t = time
      x = distance

The thermal diffusivity a in this equation is defined as

$$a = \frac{\lambda}{\varrho\, c_{\mathrm{p}}} \tag{4.2.2}$$

where λ = thermal conductivity
      c_{p} = specific heat at constant pressure
      ρ = density

The numerical solution of Eq. (4.2.1) is treated in the Section 6.3.4. For commonly occurring geometrical shapes analytical expressions for transient conduction are given in the following sections.

4.2.1   Temperature Distribution in One-dimensional Solids

The expression for the heating or cooling of an infinite plate [2] follows from Eq. (4.2.1) (Fig. 4.7):

$$\frac{T_{\mathrm{w}} - \bar{T}_{\mathrm{b}}}{T_{\mathrm{w}} - T_{\mathrm{a}}} = \frac{8}{\pi^2}\left(\mathrm{e}^{-a_1 F_0} + \frac{1}{9}\, \mathrm{e}^{-9\, a_1 \cdot F_0} + \frac{1}{25}\, \mathrm{e}^{-25 \cdot a_1 \cdot F_0} + \ldots \right) \tag{4.2.3}$$

The Fourier number F_0 is defined by

$$F_0 = \frac{a \cdot t_{\mathrm{k}}}{X^2} \tag{4.2.4}$$

where T_{w} = constant surface temperature of the plate
      T_{a} = initial temperature
      $\bar{T}_{\mathrm{b}}$ = average temperature of the plate at time t_{T}
      t_{k} = heating or cooling time

      X = half thickness of the plate $\left[X = \dfrac{s}{2} \right]$
      $a_1 = (\pi/2)^2$
      a = thermal diffusivity, Eq. (4.2.2)

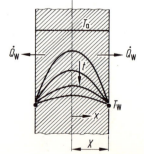

Fig. 4.7   Unsteady-state conduction in an infinite plate

The equation for an infinite cylinder with the radius r_m is given by [2]

$$\frac{T_w - \bar{T}_b}{T_w - T_a} = 0.692\, e^{-5.78 F_0} + 0.131\, e^{-30.5 F_0} + 0.0534\, e^{-74.9 F_0} + \ldots \tag{4.2.5}$$

and for a sphere with the radius r_m

$$\frac{T_w - \bar{T}_b}{T_w - T_a} = 0.608\, e^{-9.87 F_0} + 0.152\, e^{-39.5 F_0} + 0.0676\, e^{-88.8 F_0} + \ldots \tag{4.2.6}$$

where

$$F_0 = \frac{a \cdot t_k}{r_m^2} \tag{4.2.7}$$

In the range $F_0 > 1$ only the first term of these equations is significant. Therefore we obtain for the heating or cooling time [2].

plate:

$$t_K = \frac{1}{a} \cdot \left(\frac{s}{\pi}\right)^2 \ln\left[\left(\frac{8}{\pi^2}\right)\left(\frac{T_w - T_a}{T_w - \bar{T}_b}\right)\right] \tag{4.2.8}$$

cylinder:

$$t_k = \frac{r_m^2}{5.78\, a} \ln\left[0.692\left(\frac{T_w - T_a}{T_w - \bar{T}_b}\right)\right] \tag{4.2.9}$$

sphere:

$$t_k = \frac{r_m^2}{9.87\, a} \cdot \ln\left[0.608\left(\frac{T_w - T_a}{T_w - \bar{T}_b}\right)\right] \tag{4.2.10}$$

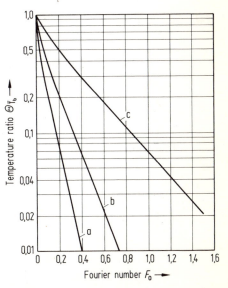

Fig. 4.8   Average temperature of an infinite slab (c), a long cylinder (b) and a sphere (a) during unsteady heating of cooling [2]

The solutions of the Eqns. (4.2.3) to (4.2.7) are presented in a semi-logarithmic plot in Fig. 4.8, in which the temperature ratio $\theta_{T_b} = (T_w - \bar{T}_b)/(T_w - T_0)$ is shown as a function of the Fourier number F_0.

Excepting small Fourier numbers these plots are straight lines approximated by the Equations (4.2.8) to (4.2.10).

If the time t_k is based on the centre-line temperature T_b instead of the average temperature $\bar{T}_b$, then we get [3]

$$t_K = \frac{s^2}{\pi^2 \cdot a} \cdot \ln\left[\frac{4}{\pi}\left(\frac{T_w - T_a}{T_w - T_b}\right)\right] \qquad (4.2.11)$$

Analogous to Fig. 4.8 the ratio θ_{T_b} with the centre-line temperature T_b at time t_k is plotted in Fig. 4.9 over the Fourier number for bodies of different geometry [4].

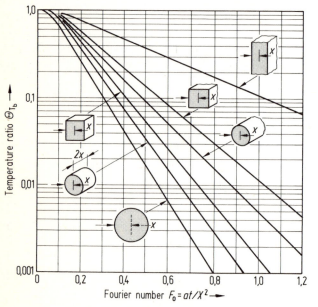

Fig. 4.9 Axis temperature for multidimensional bodies [4]

The foregoing equations apply to the case, in which the thermal resistance between the body and the surroundings is negligibly small ($\alpha_0 \to \infty$), for instance in injection molding between the part and the coolant. This means that the Biot number should be very large, $Bi \to \infty$. The Biot number for a plate is

$$Bi_{\text{plate}} = \frac{\alpha_a \cdot X}{\lambda} \qquad (4.2.12)$$

where α_a = heat-transfer coefficient of the fluid
          λ = thermal conductivity of the plastic

As the heat-transfer coefficient α_a in practice has a finite value, the temperature ratio Θ_{T_b} based on the centre-line temperature is given in Fig. 4.10 as a function of the Fourier number with the reciprocal of Biot number as parameter [5].

Example 1 [6]:

Cooling of a part in an injection mold for the following conditions:

resin: PE-LD
          thickness of the plate $s = 12.7$ mm
          temperatur of the melt $T_a = 243.3\ °C$
          mold temperature $T_w = 21.1\ °C$
          demolding temperature $T_b = 76.7\ °C$
          thermal diffusivity $a = 1.29 \times 10^{-3}\ cm^2/s$

The cooling time t_k is to be calculated.

Solution:

The temperature ratio Θ_{T_b}:

$$\Theta_{T_b} = \frac{T_b - T_w}{T_a - T_w} = \frac{76.7 - 21.1}{243.3 - 21.1} = 0.25$$

Fourier number F_0 from Fig. 4.9 at $\Theta_{T_b} = 0.25$

$$F_0 = 0.65$$

cooling time t_k:

$$X = \frac{s}{2} = \frac{12.7}{2} = 6.35\ \text{mm}.$$

$$F_0 = \frac{a \cdot t_K}{X^2} = \frac{1.29 \cdot 10^{-3} * t_K}{(0.635)^2} = 0.65$$

$$t_k = 203\ s$$

Example 2 [6]:

Calculate the cooling time t_k in the Example 1 if the mold is cooled by a coolant having a heat-transfer coefficient $\alpha_a = 2839\ W/(m^2 \cdot K)$.

Solution:

$$\alpha_a = 2839\ W/(m^2 \cdot K)$$

$$\lambda_{plastic} = 0.242\ W/(m \cdot K)$$

The resulting Biot number is

$$Bi = \frac{\alpha_a \cdot X}{\lambda} = \frac{2839 \cdot 6.35}{0.242 \cdot 1000} = 74.49 \qquad\qquad \frac{1}{Bi} = 0.01342$$

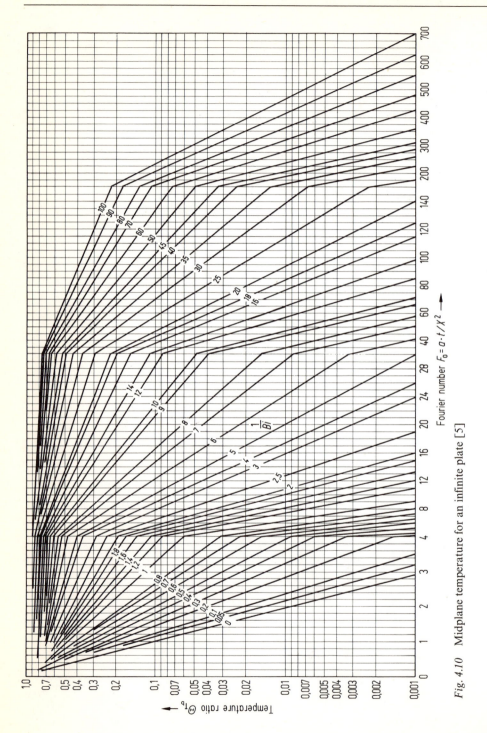

Fig. 4.10   Midplane temperature for an infinite plate [5]

As can be read from Fig. 4.10 the Fourier number does not differ much from the one in the previous example for $\Theta_{T_b}=0.25$ and $1/Bi=0.01342$. The resistance due to convection is therefore negligible and the cooling time remains almost the same.

However, the convection resistance has to be taken into account in the case of a film, 127 µ thick cooling in quiescent air, as the following calculation shows:

The heat-transfer coefficient α_a for this case is approximately

$$\alpha_a = 56.78 \ \text{W}/(\text{m}^2 \cdot \text{K})$$

The Biot number Bi_t

$$Bi = \frac{56.78 \cdot 63.5}{10^6 \cdot 0.242} = 0.0149$$

$$\frac{1}{Bi} = 67.1$$

F_0 from Fig. 4.10

$$F_0 = 95$$

The cooling time

$$t_k = \frac{X^2 \cdot F_0}{a} = \frac{63.5^2 \cdot 10^3 \cdot 95}{10^8 \cdot 1.29} = 2.97 \ \text{s}$$

Example 3 [7]:

Cooling of an extruded wire

A wire of polyacetal of diameter 3.2 mm is extruded at 190 °C into a water bath at 20 °C. Calculate the length of the water bath to cool the wire from 190 °C to a centre-line temperature of 140 °C.

The following conditions are given:

$$\alpha_a = 1700 \ \text{W}/(\text{m}^2 \cdot \text{K})$$
$$a_{\text{plastic}} = 10^{-7} \ \text{m}^2/\text{s}$$
$$\lambda_{\text{plastic}} = 0.23 \ \text{W}/(\text{m} \cdot \text{K})$$

haul-off rate of the wire $V_H = 0.5 \ \text{m/s}$

Solution:

The Biot number $Bi = \dfrac{\alpha_a \cdot R}{\lambda}$

where $R = $ radius of the wire

$$Bi = \frac{1700 \cdot 1.6}{1000 \cdot 0.23} = 11.13 \qquad\qquad \frac{1}{Bi} = 0.0846$$

The temperature ratio Θ_{T_b}:

$$\Theta_{T_b} = \frac{(T_b - T_w)}{(T_a - T_w)} = \frac{140 - 20}{190 - 20} = \frac{120}{170} = 0.706$$

The Fourier number F_0 for $\Theta_{T_b} = 0.706$ and $\dfrac{1}{Bi} = 0.0846$ from Fig. 4.10 is roughly

$$F_0 \approx 0.16$$

The cooling time t_k follows from

$$\frac{a \cdot t_k}{R^2} = \frac{10^{-7} \cdot t_k}{(1.6 \cdot 10^{-3})^2} = \frac{t_k}{2.56 \cdot 10} = 0.16$$

$$t_k = 4.1 \text{ s}$$

The length of the water bath is

$$V_H \cdot t_k = 0.5 \cdot 4.1 = 2.05 \text{ m}$$

4.2.2   Thermal Contact Temperature

If two semi-infinite bodies of different initial temperatures θ_{A_1} and θ_{A_2} are brought into contact as indicated in Fig. 4.11 the resulting contact temperature θ_K is given by [3]

$$\theta_K = \frac{\theta_A + \dfrac{(\sqrt{\lambda \varrho c})_2}{(\sqrt{\lambda \varrho c})_1} \theta_{A_2}}{1 + \dfrac{(\sqrt{\lambda \varrho c})_2}{(\sqrt{\lambda \varrho c})_1}} \tag{4.2.13}$$

where λ = thermal conductivity
$\quad\quad\quad \varrho$ = density
$\quad\quad\quad c$ = specific heat
$\sqrt{\lambda \varrho c}$ = coefficient of heat penetration

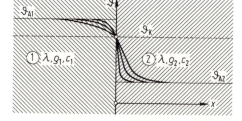

Fig. 4.11   Temperature distribution in semi-infinite solids in contact [3]

Eq. (4.2.13) applies to the case of contact of short duration of thick bodies also. It follows from this equation, that the contact temperature depends on the ratio of the coefficients of heat penetration and lies nearer to the initial temperature of that body, which has a higher coefficient of penetration. The ratio of the temperature differences $(\theta_{A_1} - \theta_K)$ and $(\theta_K - \theta_{A_2})$ are inversely proportional to the coefficient of penetration:

$$\frac{\theta_{A_1} - \theta_K}{\theta_K - \theta_{A_2}} = \frac{(\sqrt{\lambda \varrho c})_2}{(\sqrt{\lambda \varrho c})_1} \tag{4.2.14}$$

Example:

The contact temperature $\theta_{w_{max}}$ of the wall of an injection mold at the time of injection is according to Eq. (4.2.13) [8]

$$\theta_{w_{max}} = \frac{b_w \, \theta_{w_{min}} + b_p \, \theta_M}{b_w + b_p} \tag{4.2.15}$$

where $b = \sqrt{\lambda \varrho c}$
$\theta_{w_{min}}$ = temperature before injection
θ_M = melt temperature

Indices w and p refer to mold and polymer, respectively.

As shown in Table 4.1 [8] the coefficients of heat penetration of metals are much higher than those of polymer melts. Hence the contact temperature lies in the vicinity of the mold wall temperature before injection.

Table 4.1   Coefficients of heat penetration of mold material and resin [8]

Material	Coefficient of heat penetration b $(Ws^{0.5} \cdot m^{-2} \cdot K^{-1})$
Beryllium Copper (BeCu 25)	$17.2 \cdot 10^3$
Unalloyed Steel (C45W3)	$13.8 \cdot 10^3$
Chromium Steel (X40Cr13)	$11.7 \cdot 10^3$
Polyethylene (PE-HD)	$0.99 \cdot 10^3$
Polystyrene (PS)	$0.57 \cdot 10^3$

The values given in the Table 4.1 refer to the following units of the properties:

thermal conductivity λ: W/(m·K)
density ϱ: kg/m³
specific heat c: kJ/(kg·K)

The approximate values for steel are

$\lambda = 50$ W/(m·K)
$\varrho = 7850$ kg/m³
$c = 0.485$ kJ/(kg·K)

The coefficient of heat penetration b

$$b = \sqrt{\lambda \cdot \varrho \cdot c} = \sqrt{50 \cdot 7.85 \cdot 10^3 \cdot 0.485 \cdot 10^3} = 13.8 \cdot 10^3 \; Ws^{0.5} \cdot m^{-2} \cdot K^{-1}$$

4.3   Heat Conduction with Dissipation

The power created by the tangential forces in the control volume of the fluid flow is denoted as dissipation [9]. In shear flow the rate of energy dissipation per unit volume is equal to the product of shear force and shear rate [10]. The power due to dissipation [11] is therefore

$$\dot{E}_d = \tau \dot{\gamma} \qquad (4.3.1)$$

From Eq. (2.3.8) for the power law we get

$$\dot{E}_d = \left(\frac{1}{K}\right)^{\frac{1}{n}} \cdot \dot{\gamma}^{\frac{1}{n}+1} \qquad (4.3.2)$$

For a Newtonian fluid with $n=1$ we obtain

$$\dot{E}_d = \eta \dot{\gamma}^2 \qquad (4.3.3)$$

The applicable differential equation for a melt flow between two plates, where the upper plate is moving with a velocity U_x (Fig. 2.4) and the lower plate is stationary [11] is

$$\lambda \frac{\partial^2 T}{\partial y^2} + \eta \left(\frac{\partial u_x}{\partial y}\right)^2 = 0 \qquad (4.3.4)$$

For drag flow the velocity gradient is given by

$$\frac{\partial u}{\partial y} = \frac{U_x}{H} \qquad (4.3.5)$$

Eq. (4.3.4) can now be written as

$$\lambda \frac{\partial^2 T}{\partial y^2} = -\eta \frac{U_x^2}{H^2} \qquad (4.3.6)$$

If the temperature of the upper plate is T_1 and that of lower plate T_0 the temperature profile of the melt is obtained by integrating Eq. (4.3.6). The resulting expression is

$$T = \frac{\eta U_x^2 \cdot y}{2\lambda H}\left(1 - \frac{y}{H}\right) + \frac{y}{H}(T_1 - T_0) + T_0 \qquad (4.3.7)$$

As shown in Section 6.2.3 this equation can be used to calculate the temperature of the melt film in an extruder.

4.4   Dimensionless Groups

Dimensionless groups can be used to describe complicated processes which are influenced by a large number of variables with the advantage that the whole process can be analysed on a sound basis by means of a few dimensionless parameters. Their use in correlating experimental data and in scaling-up of equipment is well known.

Table 4.2 shows some of the dimensionless groups which are often used in plastics engineering.

Table 4.2   Dimensionless Groups

Symbol	Name	Definition
Bi	Biot number	$\alpha_a\, l/\lambda_i$
Br	Brinkman number	$\eta\, w^2/(\lambda \Delta T)$
Deb	Deborah number	t_D/t_p
F_0	Fourier number	at/l^2
Gr	Grashof number	$g\beta \cdot \Delta T\, l^3/v^2$
Gz	Graetz number	$l^2/(a \cdot t_v)$
Le	Lewis number	a/δ
Na	Nahme number	$\beta_T\, w^2\, \eta/\lambda$
Nu	Nusselt number	$\alpha l/\lambda$
Pe	Peclet number	wl/a
Pr	Prandtl number	v/a
Re	Reynolds number	$\varrho\, wl/\eta$
Sh	Sherwood number	$\beta_s\, l/\delta$
Sc	Schmidt number	v/δ
Sk	Stokes number	$P \cdot l/(\eta \cdot w)$

Nomenclature:

a:	thermal diffusivity	(m^2/s)
g:	acceleration due to gravity	(m/s^2)
l:	characteristic length	(m)
p:	pressure	(N/m^2)
t:	time	(s)

Indices D, P: memory and process of polymer respectively

ΔT:	temperature difference	(K)
w:	velocity of flow	(m/s)
α_a:	outside heat-transfer coefficient	$[W/(m^2 \cdot K)]$
β:	coefficient of volumetric expansion	(K^{-1})
β_T:	temperature coefficient in the power law of viscosity according to Eq. (2.3.14)	(K^{-1})
β_s:	mass transfer coefficient	(m/s)
δ:	diffusion coefficient	(m^2/s)
η:	viscosity	$\left(\dfrac{N}{m^2} \cdot s\right)$
λ:	thermal conductivity (Index i refers to the inside value)	$[W/(m \cdot K)]$
v:	kinematic viscosity	(m^2/s)
t_v:	residence time	(s)
ϱ:	density	(kg/m^3)

4.4.1 Physical Meaning of Dimensionless Groups

Biot number: Ratio of thermal resistances in series: $(l/\lambda_i)/(1/\alpha_a)$;
application: heating or cooling of solids by heat transfer through conduction and convection.

Brinkmann number: ratio of heat dissipated (ηw^2) lto heat conducted $(\lambda \Delta T)$;
application: polymer melt flow (Section 6.3.6.1).

Fourier number: ratio of a characteristic body dimension to an approximate temperature-wave penetration depth for a given time [16];
application: unsteady-state heat conduction.

Deborah number: ratio of the period of memory of the polymer to the duration of processing [13]. At $Deb > 1$ the process is determined by the elasticity of the material, whereas at $Deb < 1$ the viscous behavior of the polymer influences the process remarkably.

Grashof number: ratio of the buoyant force $g\beta \Delta T l^3$ to frictional force (v);
application: heat transfer by free convection.

Graetz number: ratio of the time to reach thermal equilibrium perpendicular to the flow direction (l^2/a) to the residence time (t_v);
application: heat transfer to fluids in motion.

Lewis number: ratio of thermal diffusivity (a) to the diffusion coefficient (δ);
application: phenomena with simultaneous heat and mass transfer.

Nusselt number: ratio of the total heat transferred $(\alpha \cdot l)$ to the heat by conduction (λ);
application: convective heat transfer.

Peclet number: ratio of heat transfer by convection $(\varrho c_p \cdot w \cdot l)$ to the heat by conduction (λ);
application: heat transfer by forced convection.

Nahme or Griffith number: ratio of viscous dissipation $(\beta_T w^2 \eta)$ to the heat by conduction (λ) perpendicular to the direction of flow;
application: heat transfer in melt flow.

Prandtl number: ratio of the kinematic viscosity (v) to thermal diffusivity (a);
application: convective heat transfer.

Reynolds number: ratio of the inertial force $(\varrho w l)$ to viscous force (η);
application: The Reynolds number serves as a criterium to judge the type of flow. In pipe flow, when Re is less than 2300 the flow is laminar. The flow is turbulent at Re greater than about 4000. Between 2100 and 4000 the flow may be laminar or turbulent depending on conditions at the entrance of the tube and on the distance from the entrance [2];
application: fluid flow and heat transfer.

Sherwood number: ratio of the resistance to diffusion (l/δ) to the resistance to mass transfer ($1/\beta_s$);
application: mass transfer problems.

Schmidt number: ratio of kinematic viscosity (v) to the diffusion coefficient (δ);
application: heat and mass transfer problems.

Stokes number: ratio of pressure forces ($p \cdot l$) to viscous forces ($\eta \cdot w$);
application: pressure flow of viscous media like polymer melts.

The use of dimensionless numbers in calculating non-Newtonian flow problems is illustrated in Section 6.3.3 with an example.

4.5 Heat Transfer by Convection

Heat-transfer by convection, particularly forced convection plays an important role in many polymer processing operations such as in cooling a blown film or a part in an injection mold, to mention only two examples.

A number of expressions is to be found in the literature on heat transfer [3] for calculating the heat-transfer coefficient α (see Section 4.1.6). The general relationship for forced convection has the form

$$Nu = f(\mathrm{Re}, \mathrm{Pr}) \tag{4.5.1}$$

The equation for the turbulent flow in a tube is given by [16]

$$Nu = 0.027 \, \mathrm{Re}^{0.8} \cdot \mathrm{Pr}^n \tag{4.5.2}$$

where $n = 0.4$ for heating
and $n = 0.3$ for cooling

The following equation applies to laminar flow in a tube with a constant wall temperature [3]

$$Nu_{\mathrm{lam}} = \sqrt[3]{3.66^3 + 1.61^3 \, \mathrm{Re} \cdot \mathrm{Pr} \cdot d_i/l} \tag{4.5.3}$$

where $d_i = $ inside tube diameter
$l = $ tube length

The expression for the laminar-flow heat transfer to flat plate is [3]

$$Nu_{\mathrm{lam}} = 0{,}664 \sqrt{\mathrm{Re}} \sqrt[3]{\mathrm{Pr}} \tag{4.5.4}$$

Eq. (4.5.4) is valid for $Pr = 0.6$ to 2000 and $Re < 10^5$.

The equation for turbulent-flow heat transfer to flat plate is given as [3]

$$Nu_{\mathrm{turb}} = \frac{0.037 \, Re^{0.8} \cdot Pr}{1 + 2.448 \, Re^{-0.1} (Pr^{2/3} - 1)} \tag{4.5.5}$$

Eq. (4.5.5) applies for the conditions:

$$Pr = 0.6 \text{ to } 2000$$

and $5 \cdot 10^5 < Re < 10^7$.

The properties of the fluids in the equations above are to be found at a mean fluid temperature.

Example:

A flat film is moving in a coating equipment at a velocity of 130 m/min on rolls which are 200 mm apart. Calculate the heat-transfer coefficient α if the surrounding medium is air at a temperature of 50 °C.

Solution:

The properties of air at 50 °C are:

kinematic viscosity $v = 17.86 \cdot 10^{-6} \, \text{m}^2/\text{s}$
thermal conductivity $\lambda = 28.22 \cdot 10^{-3} \, \text{W}/(\text{m} \cdot \text{K})$
Prandtl number $Pr = 0.69$

The Reynolds number Re_L based on the length $L = 200$ mm is

$$Re_L = 130 \cdot \frac{1}{60} \cdot 0.2/17.86 \cdot 10^{-6} = 24\,262$$

Substituting $Re_L = 24\,262$ and $Pr = 0.69$ into Eq. (4.5.4) gives

$$Nu_{lam} = 0.664 \cdot 24\,262^{0.5} \cdot 0.69^{1/3} = 91.53$$

As the fluid is in motion on both sides of the film the Nusselt number is calculated according to [3]

$$Nu = \sqrt{Nu_{lam}^2 + Nu_{turb}^2}$$

For the turbulent flow Nu_{turb} follows from Eq. (4.5.5):

$$Nu_{turb} = \frac{0.037 \cdot 24\,262^{0.8} \cdot 0.69}{1 + 2.448 \cdot 24\,262^{-0.1}(0.69^{2/3} - 1)}$$

$$Nu_{turb} = 102$$

The resulting Nusselt number Nu is

$$Nu = \sqrt{91.53^2 + 102^2} = 137$$

The heat-transfer coefficient α results from

$$\alpha = \frac{Nu \cdot \lambda}{l} = \frac{137 \cdot 28.22 \cdot 10^{-3}}{0.2} = 19.33 \, \text{W}/(\text{m}^2 \cdot \text{K})$$

4.6   Heat Transfer by Radiation

Heating by radiation is used in thermo-forming process to heat sheets or films, so that the shaping process can take place. As at temperatures above 300 °C a substantial part of the thermal radiation consists of wavelengths in the infrared range, heat transfer by radiation is also termed as infrared radiation [14]. According to the Stefan-Boltzmann law the rate of energy radiated by a black body per unit area $\dot{e}_s$ is proportional to the absolute temperature T to the fourth power (Fig. 4.12) [1]:

$$\dot{e}_s = \sigma T^4 \tag{4.6.1}$$

The Stefan-Boltzmann constant has the value

$$\sigma = 5.77 \cdot 10^{-12} \, W/(cm^2 \cdot K^4)$$

Eq. (4.6.1) can also be written as

$$\dot{e}_s = c_s \left(\frac{T}{100}\right)^4 \tag{4.6.2}$$

where $c_s = 5.77 \dfrac{W}{m^2 \cdot K^4}$.

The dependance of the black body radiation on the direction (Fig. 4.13) [1] is given by the cosine law of Lambert

$$\dot{e}_s = \dot{e}_n \cos \phi \tag{4.6.3}$$

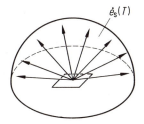

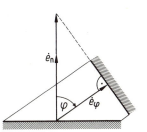

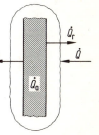

Fig. 4.12   Blackbody radiation [1]

Fig. 4.13   Lambert's law [1]

Fig. 4.14   Properties of radiation

The radiation properties of technical surfaces are defined as (Fig. 4.14) [1]:

Reflectivity $\varrho \equiv \dfrac{\dot{Q}_r}{\dot{Q}}$ (4.6.4)

Absorptivity $\alpha \equiv \dfrac{\dot{Q}_a}{\dot{Q}}$ (4.6.5)

Transmissivity $\qquad \delta \equiv \dfrac{\dot{Q}_d}{\dot{Q}}$ $\hfill$ (4.6.6)

The sum of these fractions must be unity, or

$$\varrho + \alpha + \delta = 1$$

The transmissivity δ of opaque solids is zero so that

$$\alpha + \varrho = 1$$

The reflectivity of gases ϱ is zero and for those gases which emit and absorb radiation

$$\alpha + \delta = 1$$

Real bodies emit only a fraction of the radiant energy which is emitted by a black body at the same temperature. This ratio is defined as the emissivity ε of the body,

$$\varepsilon = \frac{\dot{e}}{\dot{e}_s} \qquad (4.6.7)$$

At thermal equilibrium according to Kirchhoff's identity

$$\varepsilon = \alpha \qquad (4.6.8)$$

Radiation heat transfer between nonblack surfaces

The net rate of radiant heat exchange between two infinite parallel plates is given by [15]

$$\dot{Q}_{12} = A \varepsilon_{12} \, c_s \left[\left(\frac{T_1}{100} \right)^4 - \left(\frac{T_2}{100} \right)^4 \right] \qquad (4.6.9)$$

where A = area

ε_{12} = emissivity factor and is defined by

$$\varepsilon_{12} = \frac{1}{\dfrac{1}{\varepsilon_1} + \dfrac{1}{\varepsilon_{12}} - 1} \qquad (4.6.10)$$

Indices 1 and 2 refer to the two plates.

When T_2 is much smaller T_1 the heat flow is approximately

$$\dot{Q}_{12} = \varepsilon_1 \, c_s \, A \left(\frac{T_1}{100} \right)^4 \qquad (4.6.11)$$

When the heat transfer takes place by radiation and convection the total heat-transfer coefficient can be written as [15]

$$\alpha_{total} = \alpha_{convection} + \alpha_{radiation}$$

where

$$\alpha_{\text{radiation}} = \frac{\dot{Q}_{12}}{A(T_1 - T_2)}$$

Example:

A plastic sheet moving at a speed of 6 m/min is heated by two high temperature heating elements. Calculate the power required for heating for the following conditions, if the sheet is to be heated from 20 °C to 140 °C:

net enthalpy of the plastic for a temperature difference of 120 °C: $\Delta h = 70$ kJ/kg

width of the sheet	$w = 600$ mm
thickness	$s = 250$ μ
density of the resin	$\varrho = 900$ kg/m^3
area of the heating element	$A = 0.0093$ m^2
emissivity of the heater	$\varepsilon = 0.9$

Solution:

Heating power N_H:

Mass flow rate of the plastic $\dot{m}$:

$$\dot{m} = U \cdot w \cdot s \cdot \varrho = \frac{6*0.6*250*900}{10^6} = 0.81 \text{ kg/min}$$

$$N_H = \dot{m}\Delta h = \frac{0.81*70*1000}{60} = 945 \text{ W}$$

As the area of the heating element is small compared to that of the sheet the equation applies [14]

$$\dot{e} = \varepsilon c_s \cdot \left(\frac{T}{100}\right)^4 \frac{W}{m^2}$$

total area of the heating element $A_g = 2 \cdot A$
so that we have

$$\dot{e} A_g = N_H$$

$$0.9 * 5.77 * 2 * 0.0093 * \left(\frac{T}{100}\right)^4 = 945$$

$$\frac{T}{100} = 9.95$$

$$T = 995 \text{ K}.$$

4.7   Dielectric Heating

The dielectric heat loss which occurs in materials of low electrical conductivity, when they are placed in an electric field alternating at high frequency, is used in bonding operations for instance, to heat seal plastic sheets or films.

The power dissipated in the polymer is given by [14]

$$N_H = 2\pi f \cdot C \cdot E^2 \cdot \cot \phi \tag{4.7.1}$$

where N_H = power (W)
   f = frequency of the alternating field (s^{-1})
   C = capacitance of the polymer (farads)
   E = applied voltage (Volt)
   ϕ = phase angle

The rate of heat generation in a plastic film can be obtained from Eq. (4.7.1) and given as [15]

$$N_H = 55.7 \left(\frac{E^2 \cdot f \cdot \varepsilon_r''}{4 b^2} \right) \tag{4.7.2}$$

where N_H = rate of heat generation (W/m^3)
   ε_r'' = dielectric loss factor
   b = half thickness of the film (μ)

Example:

Given:

$$E = 500 \text{ V}$$
$$f = 10 \text{ MHz}$$
$$\varepsilon_r'' = 0.24$$
$$b = 50 \text{ }\mu$$

Calculate the rate of heat generation and the time required to heat the polymer from 20 °C to 150 °C.

Substituting the given values in Eq. (4.7.2) gives

$$N_H = \frac{55.7 * 500^2 * 10 * 10^6 * 0.24}{4 * 50^2} = 3.34 * 10^9 \text{ W/m}^3$$

The maximum heating rate ΔT per second is calculated from

$$\Delta T = \frac{N_H}{c_p \cdot \varrho} \tag{4.7.3}$$

For

$$N_H = 3.39 \cdot 10^9 \text{ W/m}^2$$
$$c_p = 2.2 \text{ kJ/(kg} \cdot \text{K)}$$

$$\rho = 800 \text{ kg/m}^3$$
$$\Delta T = \frac{3.39 \cdot 10^6}{800 \cdot 2.2} = 1926 \text{ K/s}$$

Finally the heating time

$$t = \frac{(150 - 20)}{1926} = 0.067 \text{ s}$$

4.8   Fick's Law of Diffusion

Analogous to Fourier's law of heat conduction (Eq. (4.1.1)) and the equation for shear stress in shear flow (Eq. (2.3.4)) the diffusion rate in mass transfer is given by Fick's law. This can be written as [16]

$$\frac{\dot{m}_A}{A} = -D_{AB} \frac{\partial c_A}{\partial x} \tag{4.8.1}$$

where $\dot{m}_A$ = mass flux per unit time
A = Area
D_{AB} = diffusion coefficient of the constituent A in constituent B
c_A = mass concentration of component A per unit volume
x = distance.

The governing expression for the transient rate of diffusion is [2]

$$\frac{\partial c_A}{\partial t} = D_{AB} \frac{\partial^2 c_A}{\partial x^2} \tag{4.8.2}$$

where t = time
x = distance.

The desorption of volatile or gaseous components from a molten polymer in an extruder can be calculated from [17] using Eq. (4.8.2)

$$R_1 = A_c C_0 \sqrt{\frac{4 \cdot D}{\pi \cdot t}} \tag{4.8.3}$$

where R_1 = rate of desorption (g/s)
A_e = area of desorption (cm^2)
C_0 = initial concentration of the volatile component (g/cm^3) in the polymer
D = diffusion coefficient (cm^2/s)
t = time of exposure (s) of the polymer to the surrounding atmosphere

4.8.1   Permeability

Plastics are to some extent permeable to gases, vapors and liquids. The diffusional characteristics of polymers can be described in terms of a quantity known as permeability.

The mass of the fluid permeating through the polymer at equilibrium conditions is given by [7]

$$m = \frac{P \cdot t \cdot A \cdot (p_1 - p_2)}{s} \qquad (4.8.4)$$

m = mass of the fluid permeating (g)

p = permeability $\left[\dfrac{g}{m \cdot s \cdot Pa}\right]$

t = time of diffusion (s)
A = Area of the film or membrane (m^2)
p_1, p_2 = partial pressures on the side 1 and 2 of the film (Pa)
s = thickness of the film (m)

Besides its dependence on temperature the permeability is influenced by the difference in partial pressures of the fluid and thickness of the film. Other factors which influence permeability are the structure of the polymer film like crystallinity and the type of fluid.

4.8.2   Absorption and Desorption

The process by which the fluid is absorbed or desorbed by a plastics material is time-dependent, governed by its solubility and by the diffusion coefficient [7]. The period until equilibrium value is reached, can be very long. Its magnitude can be estimated by the half-life of the process given by [7]

$$t_{0.5} = \frac{0.04919 \cdot s^2}{D} \qquad (4.8.5)$$

where $t_{0.5}$ = half-life of the process
$\quad\quad\quad s$ = thickness of the polymer assumed to be penetrated by one side
$\quad\quad\quad D$ = diffusion coefficient

The value of $t_{0.5}$ for moisture in polymethyl methacrylate (PMMA) for $D = 0.3 \cdot 10^{-12}\, m^2/s$ and $s = 3$ mm is 17.1 days, when the sheet is wetted from one side only [7]. However, the equilibrium absorption takes much longer, as the absorption rate decreases with saturation.

Literature

[1] BENDER, E.: Lecture notes, Wärme- und Stoffübergang, Univ. Kaiserslautern (1982)
[2] MCCABE, W.L., SMITH, J.C., HARRIOTT, P.: Unit Operations of Chemical Engineering. McGraw Hill, New York (1985)
[3] MARTIN, H.: in VDI-Wärmeatlas, VDI-Verlag, Düsseldorf (1984)
[4] WELTY, J.R., WICKS, C.E., WILSON, R.E.: Fundamentals of Momentum, Heat and Mass Transfer, John Wiley, New York (1983)
[5] KREITH, F., BLACK, W.Z.: Basic Heat Transfer, Harper & Row, New York (1980)
[6] THORNE, J.L.: Plastics Process Engineering, Marcel Dekker Inc., New York (1979)
[7] OGORKIEWICZ, R.M.: Thermoplastics – Properties and Design, John Wiley, New York (1974)
[8] WÜBKEN, G.: Berechnen von Spritzgießwerkzeugen, VDI-Verlag, Düsseldorf (1974)
[9] GERSTEN, K.: Einführung in die Strömungsmechanik, Vieweg, Braunschweig (1981)
[10] WINTER, H.H.: Extruder als Plastifiziereinheit, VDI-Verlag, Düsseldorf (1977)
[11] RAUWENDAAL, C.: Polymer Extrusion, Hanser, Munich (1986)
[12] KREMER, H.: Grundlagen der Feuerungstechnik, Engler-Bunte-Institute, Univ. Karlsruhe (1964)
[13] COGSWELL, F.N.: Polymer Melt Rheology, George Godwin Ltd., London (1981)
[14] BERNHARDT, E.C.: Processing of Thermoplastic Materials, Reinhold, New York (1959)
[15] MCKELVEY, J.M.: Polymer Processing, John Wiley, New York (1962)
[16] HOLMAN, J.P.: Heat Transfer, McGraw Hill, New York (1980)
[17] SECOR, R.M.: Polymer Engineering and Science, 26 (1986) p. 647

5   Designing Plastics Parts

The deformational behavior of polymeric materials depends mainly on the type and magnitude of loading, time of application of the load and temperature. The deformation is related to these factors in a complex manner, so that the mathematical treatment of deformation requires a great computational effort [1]. However, in recent times calculational procedures for designing plastics parts have been developed using stress-strain data, which were carefully measured by employing computer aided testing of polymers [2].

5.1   Strength of Polymers

The basic equation for calculating the design stress of a part under load is given by [1]

$$\sigma_{v\text{max}} \leqq \sigma_{\text{zul}} = \frac{K}{S \cdot A} \tag{5.1.1}$$

where K = material strength as a mechanical property
$\sigma_{v\text{max}}$ = maximum stress occurring in the part
σ_{zul} = allowable stress
S = factor of safety
A = material reduction factor

The relation between allowable stress and the polymer-dependent reduction factors can be written as [1]

$$\sigma_{\text{zul}} = \frac{K}{S} \cdot \frac{1}{A_\theta} \cdot \frac{1}{A_{\text{st}}} \cdot \frac{1}{A_{\text{dyn}}} \cdot \frac{1}{A_{\text{A}}} \cdot \frac{1}{A_{\text{w}}} \dots \tag{5.1.2}$$

The factor A_θ considers the influence of temperature on the strength of material and can be calculated from [1]

$$A_\theta = \frac{1}{1 - [k(\theta - 20)]} \tag{5.1.3}$$

where θ = temperature. The limits of applicability of Eq. (5.1.3) are $20 \leqq \theta \leqq 100\,°\text{C}$.

The value k based on the reference temperature of 20 °C is given for the following materials as [1]:

PA66	= 0.0112
PA6	= 0.0125
PBT	= 0.0095
GR-PA and GR-PBT	= 0.0071
POM	= 0.0082
ABS	= 0.0117

The other reduction factors in Eq. (5.1.2) consider following effects:

The factor A_{st} represents the effect of the time of static loading and can have following values depending on time [1]:

time	hours	weeks	months	years
A_{st}	1.3	1.6	1.7	2

The factor A_{dyn} takes the effect of dynamic loading into account and lies in the range of 1.3 to 1.6.

The factor A_A considers the influence of aging and has to be determined experimentally.

The reduction of strength caused by the absorption of moisture by the plastic can be estimated from the factor A_w. For unreinforced polyamides A_w is roughly [1]

$$A_w = \frac{1}{1 - 0.22\,f} \tag{5.1.4}$$

with f lying between $0 < f < 3$

where f = weight percentage of moisture

The value of A_w is 3.4 when f is greater than 3.

5.2 Part Failure

Usually stresses resulting from the loading of the part are multiaxial. As measured material properties do not exist for combined stresses the multiaxial state has to be reduced to the uniaxial state by applying the principle of equivalence. According to HUBER, VON MISES and HENKY [1] the governing equation for the equivalent stress is

$$\sigma_{v_{HMH}} = \frac{1}{\sqrt{2}} \left[(\sigma_1 - \sigma_2)^2 + (\sigma_3 - \sigma_1)^2 + (\sigma_2 - \sigma_3)^2 \right]^{0.5} \tag{5.2.1}$$

where σ_1, σ_2 and σ_3 are normal stresses. The equivalent strain $\bar{\varepsilon}$ is defined by [3]

$$\bar{\varepsilon} = \frac{\sqrt{2}}{3} \left[(\varepsilon_1 - \varepsilon_2)^2 + (\varepsilon_2 - \varepsilon_3)^2 + (\varepsilon_3 - \varepsilon_1)^2 \right]^{0.5} \tag{5.2.2}$$

Materials, whose compressive stress is higher than the tensile stress can be better described by the conical or parabolic criterion [1]. The equivalent stress $\sigma_{v_{kon}}$ according to the conical criterion is given as [1]

$$\sigma_{v_{kon}} = \frac{1}{2m} \left[(m-1)(\sigma_1 + \sigma_2 + \sigma_3) \pm \frac{1+m}{\sqrt{2}} \right.$$
$$\left. \cdot \{ (\sigma_1 - \sigma_2)^2 + (\sigma_3 - \sigma_1)^2 + (\sigma_2 - \sigma_3)^2 \}^{0.5} \right] \tag{5.2.3}$$

The parabolic failure criterion is defined by

$$\sigma_{v\text{parab}} = \frac{m-1}{2m}(\sigma_1+\sigma_2+\sigma_3)\pm\left\{\frac{(m-1)^2}{4m^2}(\sigma_1+\sigma_2+\sigma_3)^2\right.$$

$$\left.+\frac{1}{2m}[(\sigma_1-\sigma_2)^2+(\sigma_3-\sigma_1)^2+(\sigma_2-\sigma_3)^2]\right\}^{0.5} \tag{5.2.4}$$

where m is the ratio of compressive stress to tensile stress.

Example:

Fig. 5.1 [1] shows a press fit assembly consisting of a metal shaft and a hub made out of POM. The joint strength can be determined in the following manner:

For the numerical values $\frac{r_a}{r_i}=1.6$ and $p=22\,\text{N/mm}^2$ the equivalent stress is to be calculated.

The tangential stress σ_t is given by

$$\sigma_t = p \cdot \frac{[(r_a/r_i)^2+1]}{(r_a/r_i)^2-1}$$

Substituting the values above

$$=22\cdot\frac{(1.6^2+1)}{(1.6^2-1)}=50.2\,\text{N/mm}^2 \tag{5.2.5}$$

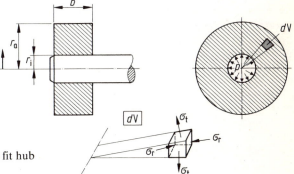

Fig. 5.1　Stress analysis in a press fit hub

The radial compressive stress σ_r is

$$\sigma_r = -p$$
$$= -22\,\text{N/mm}^2$$

Substituting $\sigma_t=50.2\,\text{N/mm}^2$, $\sigma_2=-22\,\text{N/mm}^2$ and $\sigma_3=0$ in Eq. (5.2.1) gives

$$\sigma_{v\text{HMH}} = \frac{2}{\sqrt{2}}[(50.2+22)^2+50.2^2+22^2]=64.1\,\text{N/mm}^2$$

The equivalent stress $\sigma_{v_{kon}}$ according to Eq. (5.2.3) for conical failure criterion is obtained from, with $m = 1.4$ for POM.

$$\sigma_{v_{kon}} = \frac{1}{2.8} \cdot \left[0.4(50.2 - 22) + \frac{2.4}{1.414} \right.$$

$$\left. * \{ (50.2 + 22)^2 + 50.2^2 + 22^2 \}^{0.5} \right] = 58.98 \ N/mm^2$$

The yield point of POM is around $58 \ N/mm^2$. Thus the assumed joint strength is too high. In the case of deformation of the part by shear the shear stress is given by [1]

$$\tau = 0.5\sigma \qquad\qquad\qquad (5.2.6)$$

5.3   Time-dependent Deformational Behavior

5.3.1   Short-term Stress-strain Behavior

As mentioned in Section 2.4 polymers are viscoelastic materials and their deformational behavior is nonlinear. A typical stress-strain curve of POM under short-term loading is shown in Fig. 5.2. Curves of this type can be fitted by a fifth degree polynomial of the form [4]

$$\sigma = PK_0 + PK_1 \cdot |\varepsilon| + PK_2 \cdot |\varepsilon|^2 + PK_3 \cdot |\varepsilon|^3$$

$$+ PK_4 \cdot |\varepsilon|^4 + PK_5 \cdot |\varepsilon|^5 \qquad\qquad (5.3.1)$$

where $PK_0 \ldots PK_5$ are polynomial coefficients which are dependent on the resin at a given temperature.

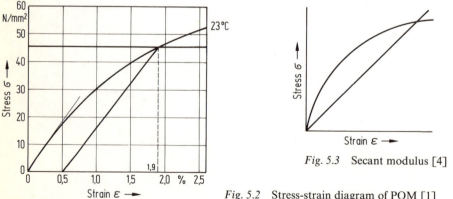

Fig. 5.3   Secant modulus [4]

Fig. 5.2   Stress-strain diagram of POM [1]

The secant modulus (Fig. 5.3) is given by

$$E_\varepsilon = \frac{\sigma}{\varepsilon} \qquad\qquad\qquad (5.3.2)$$

Setting $PK_0 = 0$ it follows from (5.3.1)

$$E_\varepsilon = PK_1 + PK_2 \cdot |\varepsilon| + PK_3 \cdot |\varepsilon|^2 + PK_4 \cdot |\varepsilon|^3 + PK_5 \cdot |\varepsilon|^4 \qquad (5.3.3)$$

The coefficients PK_1 to PK_5 are determined from measured data of stress-strain plots by means of regression analysis [5]. Thus the secant modulus can be calculated for a given strain. To represent material behavior a secant modulus with the stress $\sigma_{0.5}$ corresponding to a strain of 0.5% is also used (Fig. 5.2).

5.3.3 Long-term Stress-strain Behavior

The dimensioning of load bearing plastics components requires the knowledge of stress-strain data obtained under conditions of long term loading of polymers at different temperatures. Retardation experiments provide data on time-dependent strain in the form of creep plots, Fig. 5.4a. In Fig. 5.4b the stress is given as a function of time for different values of strain. The isochronous stress-strain-time curves are illustrated in Fig. 5.4c.

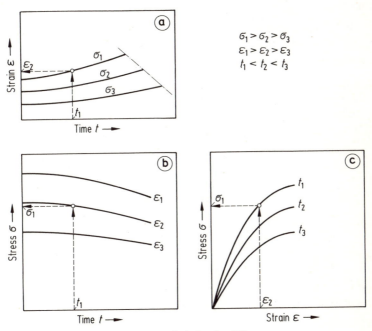

Fig. 5.4   Long-term stress-strain behavior [7]

The critical strain method according to MENGES [10] provides useful criterion for designing plastics parts. The experiments of MENGES and TAPROGGE [10] show that safe design is possible when the critical strain is taken as the allowable deformation. The corresponding tensile stress can be obtained from the isochronous stress-strain diagram.

The expression for calculating the time-dependent strain according to FINDLEY [8] is given as

$$\varepsilon(t) = A \sinh B\sigma + C \cdot t^n \sinh D\sigma \tag{5.3.4}$$

where A, B, C, D and n are material constants.

The power function of FINDLEY [2] is written as

$$\varepsilon(t) = \frac{\sigma(t)}{E_0} + m(\sigma) \cdot t^{n(\sigma)} \tag{5.3.5}$$

The function for the coefficient m is a fifth degree polynomial and that of n is a straight line. With the Findley power function the long term behavior of plastics up to 10^5 hours can be described on the basis of measurements covering shorter periods of around 10^3 hours [2].

Example [9]:

The minimum depth of the simple beam of SAN shown in Fig. 5.5 is to be determined for the following conditions:

The beam should support a mid-span load of 11.13 N for 5 years without fracture and without causing a deflection greater than 2.54 mm.

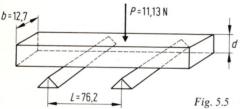

Fig. 5.5   Beam under midspan load [9]

Solution:

The maximum stress is given by

$$\sigma_{max} = \frac{1.5 \cdot P \cdot L}{b \cdot d^2} \tag{5.3.6}$$

where $P =$ load (N)

$L, b, d =$ dimensions in (mm) as shown in Fig. 5.5

The creep modulus E_c is calculated from

$$E_c = \frac{P \cdot L^3}{4 \cdot f \cdot b \cdot d^3} \tag{5.3.7}$$

where f is deflection in (mm).

The maximum stress from Fig. 5.6 at a period of 5 years $(= 43\,800$ h) is

$$\sigma_{max} = 23.44 \text{ N/mm}^2$$

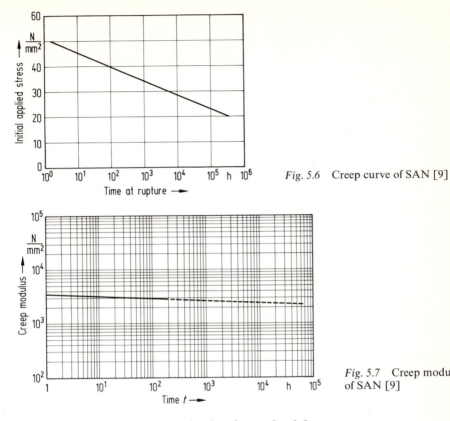

Fig. 5.6   Creep curve of SAN [9]

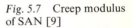

Fig. 5.7   Creep modulus
of SAN [9]

Working stress σ_w with an assumed safety factor $S = 0.5$:

$$\sigma_w = 23.44 \cdot 0.5 = 11.72 \text{ N/mm}^2$$

creep modulus E_c at $\sigma < \sigma_w$ and a period of 5 years from Fig. 5.7:

$$E_c = 2413 \text{ N/mm}^2$$

creep modulus E_c with a safety factor $S = 0.75$:

$$E_c = 2413 \cdot 0.75 = 1809.75 \text{ N/mm}^2$$

The depth of the beam results from Eq. (5.3.6)

$$d = \left(\frac{1.5 * P \cdot L}{b \cdot \sigma_{max}}\right)^{0.5} = \left(\frac{1.5 * 11.13 * 76.2}{12.7 * 11.72}\right)^{0.5} = 2.92 \text{ mm}$$

The deflection is calculated from Eq. (5.3.7)

$$f = \frac{P \cdot L^3}{4 \cdot E_c \cdot b \cdot d^3} = \frac{11.13 * 76.2^3}{4 * 1809.75 * 12.7 * 2.92^3} = 2.15 \text{ mm}$$

f is less than 2.54 mm.

Literature

[1] ERHARD, G.: Berechnen von Kunststoff-Formteilen, VDI-Verlag, Düsseldorf (1986)
[2] HAHN, H.: Berechnen von Kunststoff-Formteilen, VDI-Verlag, Düsseldorf (1986)
[3] OGORKIEWICZ, R.M.: Thermoplastics, Properties and Design, John Wiley, New York (1973)
[4] AUMER, B.: Berechnen von Kunststoff-Formteilen, VDI-Verlag, Düsseldorf (1986)
[5] RAO, N.: Designing Machines and Dies for Polymer Processing, Hanser, Munich (1981)
[6] Werkstoffblätter, BASF Kunststoffe, BASF, Ludwigshafen
[7] BERGMANN, W.: Werkstofftechnik Teil 1, Hanser, München (1984)
[8] FINDLEY, W.N.: ASTM Symposium on Plastics (1944) p. 18
[9] Design Guide, Modern Plastics Encyclopedia (1978–79)
[10] MENGES, G., TAPROGGE, R.: Kunststoff-Konstruktionen. VDI-Verlag Düsseldorf (1974)

6 Formulas for Designing Extrusion and Injection Molding Equipment

6.1 Extrusion Dies

The design of extrusion dies is based on the principles of rheology, thermodynamics and heat transfer, which have been dealt with in Chapters 2 to 4. The mechanical design of the dies is done on the basis of strength of materials. The quantities to be calculated in the main are pressure, shear rate and residence time as functions of the flow path of the melt in the die. The pressure drop is required to predict the performance of the screw. Knowledge of shear rates in the die shows whether the melt flows within the range of permissible shear rates. Undue heating of the melt can be avoided on the basis of information on the residence time of the melt in the die, which also gives an indication of the uniformity of the melt flow.

6.1.1 Calculation of Pressure Drop

The relation between volume flow rate and pressure drop of the melt in a die can be expressed in the general form as [2]

$$\dot{Q} = K G^n \Delta p^n \tag{6.1.1}$$

where $\dot{Q}$ = volume flow rate
  G = die constant
  Δp = pressure difference
  K = factor of proportionality in Eq. (2.3.8)
  n = power law exponent in Eq. (2.3.12)

It follows from Eq. (6.1.1)

$$\Delta p = \frac{\dot{Q}^{\frac{1}{n}}}{K^{\frac{1}{n}} G} \tag{6.1.2}$$

6.1.1.1 Effect of Die Geometry on Pressure Drop

The die constant G depends on the geometry of the die. Circle, slit and annulus represent the cross-sections of the flow channels of extrusion dies in most cases. G for these shapes is given by the following relationships [2].

$$G_{\text{circle}} = \left(\frac{\pi}{4}\right)^{\frac{1}{n}} \cdot \frac{R^{\frac{1}{n}+1}}{2L} \tag{6.1.3}$$

where R = Radius
  L = Length of flow channel

$$G_{\text{slit}} = \left(\frac{W}{6}\right)^{\frac{1}{n}} \cdot \frac{H^{\frac{2}{n}+1}}{2L}$$

(6.1.4)

for $\dfrac{W}{H} \geqq 20$

where H is the height of the slit and W is the width.

For $\dfrac{W}{H} < 20$, G_{slit} has to be multiplied by the correction factor F_p given in Fig. 6.1.

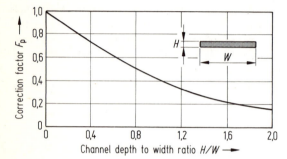

Fig. 6.1   Correction factor F_p as a function of H/W [12]

The factor F_p can be expressed as

$$F_p = 1.008 - 0.7474 \cdot \left(\frac{H}{W}\right) + 0.1638 \left(\frac{H}{W}\right)^2$$

(6.1.5)

The die constant G_{annulus} is calculated from

$$H = R_0 - R_i$$

(6.1.6)

and

$$W = \pi(R_0 + R_i)$$

(6.1.7)

where R_0 is the outer radius and R_i is the inner radius. G_{annulus} then follows from Eq. (6.1.4)

$$G_{\text{annulus}} = \left(\frac{\pi}{6}\right)^{\frac{1}{n}} \frac{(R_0 + R_i)^{\frac{1}{n}} \cdot (R_0 - R_i)^{\frac{2}{n}+1}}{2L}$$

(6.1.8)

for values of the ratio $\pi(R_0 + R_i)/(R_0 - R_i) \geqq 37$.

For smaller values of this ratio G_{annulus} has to be multiplied by the factor F_p given in Fig. 6.1. The height H and width W are obtained in this case from Eqs. (6.1.6) and (6.1.7).

6.1.1.2   Shear Rate in Die Channels

The shear rate for the different shapes of the channels treated above can be computed from [3]

$$\dot{\gamma}_{a_{\text{circle}}} = \frac{4\dot{Q}}{\pi R^3} \tag{6.1.9}$$

$$\dot{\gamma}_{a_{\text{slit}}} = \frac{6 \cdot \dot{Q}}{W \cdot H^2} \tag{6.1.10}$$

$$\dot{\gamma}_{a_{\text{annulus}}} = \frac{6 \cdot \dot{Q}}{\pi (R_0 + R_i)(R_0 - R_i)^2} \tag{6.1.11}$$

The shear rate for an equilateral triangle is given by [4]

$$\dot{\gamma}_{a_{\text{triangle}}} = \frac{10}{3} \cdot \frac{\dot{Q}}{d^3} \tag{6.1.12}$$

where d is the half length of a side of the triangle.

The relation for a quadratic cross-section is found to be [4]

$$\dot{\gamma}_{a_{\text{square}}} = \frac{3}{0.42} \cdot \frac{\dot{Q}}{a^3} \tag{6.1.13}$$

where a is the length of a side of the square.

In the case of channels with varying cross-section along the die length, for example, convergent or divergent channels, the channel is divided into a number of sufficiently small increments and the average dimensions of each increment are used in the equations given above [3].

6.1.1.3   General Relation for Pressure Drop in Any Given Channel Geometry

By means of the substitute radius defined by SCHENKEL [5] the pressure drop in cross sections other than the ones treated in the preceding sections can be calculated. The substitute radius is expressed by [5]

$$R_{\text{rh}} = \left[\frac{\left(\frac{2^{n+1}}{\pi} \right) \cdot A^{n+2}}{B^{n+1}} \right]^{\frac{1}{n+3}} \tag{6.1.14}$$

where $R_{\text{rh}} =$ substitute radius
$A =$ cross-sectional area
$B =$ circumference

6.1.1.4   Examples

The geometrical forms of the dies which occur in the following examples are illustrated in Fig. 6.2.

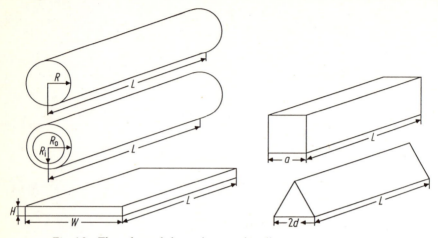

Fig. 6.2   Flow channel shapes in extrusion dies

Example 1:

It is required to calculate the pressure drop Δp of a PE-LD melt at 200 °C flowing through a round channel 100 mm long and 25 mm diameter at a mass flow rate of $\dot{m} = 10$ g/s.

The constants of viscosity in the Eq. (2.3.18) for the given PE-LD are

$$A_0 = 4.2968$$
$$A_1 = -3.4709 \cdot 10^{-1}$$
$$A_2 = -1.1008 \cdot 10^{-1}$$
$$A_3 = 1.4812 \cdot 10^{-2}$$
$$A_4 = -1.1150 \cdot 10^{-3}$$
$$b_1 = 1.29 \cdot 10^{-5}$$
$$b_2 = 4.86 \cdot 10^3 \text{ K}$$

melt density $\varrho_m = 0.7$ g/cm^3

Solution:

$$\text{Volume flow rate } \dot{Q} = \frac{\dot{m}}{\varrho_m} = \frac{10}{0.7} = 14.29 \, \frac{\text{cm}^3}{\text{s}} = 1.429 \cdot 10^{-5} \, \frac{\text{m}^3}{\text{s}}$$

Shear rate $\dot{\gamma}_a$ from Eq. (6.1.9):

$$\dot{\gamma}_a = \frac{4 \cdot \dot{Q}}{\pi \cdot R^3} = \frac{4 * 1.429 \cdot 10^{-5}}{\pi * (0.0125)^3} = 9.316 \text{ s}^{-1}$$

Shift factor a_T from Eq. (2.3.16):

$$a_T = b_1 \cdot \exp(b_2/T)$$
$$= 1.29 \cdot 10^{-5} \exp[4860/(200+273)]$$
$$= 0.374$$

The power law exponent n is, by Eq. (2.3.19),

$$\frac{1}{n} = 1 + A_1 + 2A_2 \lg(a_T \cdot \dot{\gamma}_a) + 3 \cdot A_3 (\lg(a_T \cdot \dot{\gamma}_a))^2 + 4A_4 (\lg(a_T \cdot \dot{\gamma}_a))^3$$

Substituting the constants $A_1 \dots A_4$ results in

$$n = 1.832$$

Viscosity η_a from Eq. (2.3.18):

$$\lg \eta_a = \lg a_T + A_0 + A_1 \lg(a_T \cdot \dot{\gamma}_a) + A_2 (\lg(a_T \cdot \dot{\gamma}_a))^2$$
$$+ A_3 (\lg(a_T \cdot \dot{\gamma}_a))^3 + A_4 (\lg(a_T \cdot \dot{\gamma}_a))^4$$

with $a_T = 0.374$, $\dot{\gamma}_a = 9.316$ and the constants $A_0 \dots A_4$ we get

$$\lg \eta_a = 3.6514$$
$$\eta_a = 4481 \text{ Pa} \cdot \text{s}$$

Shear stress τ from Eq. (2.3.4):

$$\tau = \eta_a \cdot \dot{\gamma}_a = 4481 * 9.316 = 41\,745 \text{ N/m}^2$$

Factor of proportionality K from Eq. (2.3.8):

$$K = \frac{\dot{\gamma}_a}{\tau^n} = 3.194 * 10^{-8}$$

Die constant G_{circle} from Eq. (6.1.3):

$$G_{circle} = \left(\frac{\pi}{4}\right)^{\frac{1}{n}} \cdot \frac{R^{\frac{3}{n}+1}}{2L}$$

$$= \left(\frac{\pi}{4}\right)^{\frac{1}{1.832}} \frac{(0.0125)^{\frac{3}{1.832}+1}}{2*(0.1)} = 4.19 * 10^{-5}$$

Pressure drop from Eq. (6.1.2):

$$\Delta p = \frac{\dot{Q}^{\frac{1}{n}}}{K^{\frac{1}{n}} \cdot G_{circle}}$$

$$= \frac{(1.429 * 10^{-5})^{\frac{1}{1.832}}}{(3.194 * 10^{-8})^{\frac{1}{1.832}} * 4.19 * 10^{-5}} = 668\,447 \text{ Pa}$$

$$= 6.68 \text{ bar}$$

Example 2:

Melt flow through a slit of width $W = 75$ mm, height $H = 1$ mm and length $L = 100$ mm.

The resin is PE-LD with the same viscosity constants as in Example 1. The mass flow rate and the melt temperature have the same values, $\dot{m} = 10$ g/s and $T = 200$ °C. The pressure drop Δp is to be calculated.

Solution:

$$\text{Volume flow rate } \dot{Q} = \frac{\dot{m}}{\varrho_m} = \frac{0.01}{700} = 1.429 * 10^{-5} \, \text{m}^3/\text{s}$$

Shear rate from Eq. (6.1.10):

$$\dot{\gamma}_a = \frac{6 \cdot \dot{Q}}{WH^2} = \frac{6 * 1.429 \cdot 10^{-5}}{0.075 * (0.001)^2} = 1143.2 \, \text{s}^{-1}$$

Shift factor a_T from Eq. (2.3.16):

$$a_T = 0.374$$

power law exponent n from Eq. (2.3.19):

$$n = 3.334$$

Viscosity η_a from Eq. (2.3.18):

$$\eta_a = 257.6 \, \text{Pa} \cdot \text{s}$$

Shear stress τ from Eq. (2.3.4):

$$\tau = 294\,524.9 \, \text{N/m}^2$$

Proportionality factor K from Eq. (2.3.8):

$$K = 6.669 * 10^{-16}$$

Correction factor F_p:

$$\frac{W}{H} = 75$$

As the ratio $\dfrac{W}{H}$ is greater than 20, the die constant which can be calculated from Eq. (6.1.4) need not be corrected.

$$G_{\text{slit}} = 2.1295 * 10^{-5}$$

and finally the pressure drop Δp from Eq. (6.1.2)

$$\Delta p = 588.8 \, \text{bar}$$

Example 3:

Melt flow through a slit width $W = 25$ mm, height $H = 5$ mm and length $L = 100$ mm.

The resin is PE-LD with the same viscosity constants as in Example 1. The mass flow rate is $\dot{m} = 10$ g/s and the melt temperature T is 200 °C. The pressure drop Δp is to be calculated.

Solution:

$$\text{Volume flow rate } \dot{Q} = \frac{\dot{m}}{\varrho_m} = \frac{0.01}{700} = 1.429 * 10^{-5} \, \text{m}^3/\text{s}$$

Shear rate $\dot{\gamma}_a$ from Eq. (6.1.10):

$$\dot{\gamma}_a = 137.2 \, \text{s}^{-1}$$

Shift factor a_T from Eq. (2.3.16):

$$a_T = 0.374$$

Power law exponent n from Eq. (2.3.19):

$$n = 2.604$$

Viscosity η_a from Eq. (2.3.18):

$$\eta_a = 1044.7 \, \text{Pa} \cdot \text{s}$$

Shear stress τ from Eq. (2.3.4):

$$\tau = 143\,318.9 \, \text{N/m}^2$$

Proportionality factor K from Eq. (2.3.8):

$$K = 5.132 * 10^{-12}$$

Correction factor F_p:

As the ratio $\dfrac{W}{H} = 5$ which is less than 20, the die constant G_{slit} has to be corrected.

F_p from Eq. (6.1.5):

$$F_p = 1.008 - 0.7474 * 0.2 + 0.1638 * 0.2^2 = 0.865$$

$$G_{\text{slit}} = 5.208 * 10^{-5}$$

$$G_{\text{slit corrected}} = 5.208 * 10^{-5} * F_p$$

$$= 4.505 * 10^{-5}$$

Pressure drop Δp from Eq. (6.1.2):

$$\Delta p = 66.24 \, \text{bar}$$

Example 4:

Melt flow through an annulus with an outside radius $R_0 = 40$ mm, an inside radius $R_i = 39$ mm and of length $L = 100$ mm.

The resin is PE-LD with the same viscosity constants as in Example 1. The process parameters, mass flow rate and melt temperature remain the same.

Solution:

$$\text{Volume flow rate } \dot{Q} = \frac{\dot{m}}{\varrho_m} = \frac{0.01}{700} = 1.429 * 10^{-5} \text{ m}^3/\text{s}$$

Shear rate $\dot{\gamma}_a$ from Eq. (6.1.11):

$$\dot{\gamma}_a = \frac{6\dot{Q}}{\pi (R_0 + R_i)(R_0 - R_i)^2}$$

$$= \frac{6 * 1.429 * 10^{-5}}{\pi (0.04 + 0.039)(0.001)^2} = 345.47 \text{ s}^{-1}$$

Shift factor a_T from Eq. (2.3.16):

$$a_T = 0.374$$

Power law exponent n from Eq. (2.3.19):

$$n = 2.907$$

Viscosity η_a from Eq. (2.3.18):

$$\eta_a = 579.43 \text{ Pa} \cdot \text{s}$$

Shear stress τ from Eq. (2.3.4):

$$\tau = 200\,173.6 \text{ N/m}^2$$

Factor of proportionality K from Eq. (2.3.8):

$$K = 1.34 \cdot 10^{-13}$$

Correction factor F_p:

As the ratio $\dfrac{\pi (R_0 + R_i)}{(R_0 - R_i)} = 248.19$ is greater than 37, no correction is necessary.

G_{annulus} from Eq. (6.1.8):

$$G_{\text{annulus}} = \left(\frac{\pi}{6}\right)^{\frac{1}{n}} \cdot (R_0 + R_i)^{\frac{1}{n}} \cdot \frac{(R_0 - R_i)^{\frac{2}{n}+1}}{2L}$$

$$= \frac{\left(\dfrac{\pi}{6}\right)^{\frac{1}{2.907}} \cdot (0.04 + 0.039)^{\frac{1}{2.907}} \cdot (0.001)^{\frac{2}{2.907}+1}}{2 * 0.1}$$

$G_{annulus} = 1.443 * 10^{-5}$

Pressure drop Δp from Eq. (6.1.2):

$$\Delta p = 400.26 \text{ bar}$$

Example 5:

Melt flow through a quadratic cross-section with the length of a side $a = 2.62$ mm. The channel length L is 50 mm.

The resin is PE-LD with the following constants occuring in the power law relation Eq. (2.3.14):

$$\eta_a = K_{OR} \exp(-\beta \cdot T) \cdot \gamma^{n_R - 1}$$

$K_{OR} = 135990$

$\beta = 0.00863$

$n_R = 0.3286$

Following conditions are given:

mass flow rate $\quad \dot{m} = 0.01$ g/s
melt temperature $\quad T = 200$ °C
melt density $\quad \varrho_m = 0.7$ g/cm^3

The pressure drop Δp is to be calculated.

Solution:

Three methods of calculation will be presented for this example.

Method a:

In this method the melt viscosity is calculated according to the power law. The method of calculation is otherwise the same as depicted in the foregoing examples.

$$\text{Volume flow rate } \dot{Q} = \frac{\dot{m}}{\varrho_m} = \frac{0.01}{0.7} = 0.014286 \ \frac{\text{cm}^3}{\text{s}}$$

$$\text{Shear rate } \dot{\gamma}_a = \frac{6\dot{Q}}{WH^2}$$

For a square with $W = H$ the shear rate $\dot{\gamma}_a$ is

$$\dot{\gamma}_a = \frac{6\dot{Q}}{H^3} = \frac{6 * 0.014286}{(0.262)^3} = 4.766 \text{ s}^{-1}$$

Power law exponent n:

$$n = \frac{1}{n_R} = \frac{1}{0.3286} = 3.043$$

Viscosity η_a from Eq. (2.3.14):

$$\eta_a = K_R \exp(-\beta \cdot T) \cdot \dot{\gamma}^{n_R - 1}$$
$$= 135\,990 \cdot \exp(-0.00863 * 200) \cdot 4.766^{(0.3286 - 1)}$$
$$= 24\,205.54 * 4.706^{0.3286 - 1}$$
$$= 8484 \, \text{Pa} \cdot \text{s}$$

Shear stress τ from Eq. (2.3.4):

$$\tau = 40\,434.88 \, \text{N/m}^2$$

Proportionality factor K from Eq. (2.3.8):

$$K = 4.568 \cdot 10^{-14}$$

Correction factor F_p:

As $\dfrac{W}{H} = 1$ is less than 20, the correction factor is obtained from Eq. (6.1.5)

$$F_p = 1.008 - 0.7474 * 1 + 0.1638 * 1^2$$
$$= 0.4244$$

Die constant G_{slit} from Eq. (6.1.4):

$$G_{slit} = 4.22 * 10^{-5}$$
$$G_{slit\,corrected} = 0.4244 * 4.22 \cdot 10^{-5}$$
$$= 1.791 \cdot 10^{-5}$$

Pressure drop Δp from Eq. (6.1.2):

$$\Delta p = 35.7 \, \text{bar}$$

Method b:

The shear rate $\dot{\gamma}_a$ is calculated from Eq. (6.1.13)

$$\dot{\gamma}_a = \frac{3}{0.42} \cdot \frac{\dot{Q}}{a^3} = \frac{3000 * 0.014286}{0.42 * 2.62^3} = 5.674 \, \text{s}^{-1}$$

Viscosity η_a from Eq. (2.3.14):

$$\eta_a = 24\,205.54 * 5.674^{0.3286 - 1} = 7546.64 \, \text{Pa} \cdot \text{s}$$

Shear stress τ from Eq. (2.3.4):

$$\tau = 42\,819.6 \, \text{N/m}^2$$

Power law exponent n from Eq. (2.3.10):

$$n = \frac{1}{n_R} = 3.043$$

Proportionality factor K from Eq. (2.3.8):

$$K = 4.568 \cdot 10^{-14}$$

The pressure drop Δp is found from

$$\Delta p_{\text{square}} = \frac{2}{K^{\frac{1}{n}}} \cdot \left(\frac{3}{0.42}\right)^{\frac{1}{n}} \cdot \frac{\dot{Q}^{\frac{1}{n}}}{a^{\frac{3}{n}+1}} \cdot 2L \qquad (6.1.15)$$

with the die constant G_{square}

$$G_{\text{square}} = \frac{1}{2}\left(\frac{0.42}{3}\right)^{\frac{1}{n}} \cdot \frac{a^{\frac{3}{n}+1}}{2L} \qquad (6.1.16)$$

$$G_{\text{square}} = \frac{1}{4} \cdot \left(\frac{0.42}{3}\right)^{\frac{1}{3.043}} \cdot \left(\frac{2.62}{1000}\right)^{\frac{3}{3.043}+1} \cdot \frac{1}{0.05}$$

$$= 1.956 \cdot 10^{-5}$$

In the Eq. (6.1.15)

$$K^{\frac{1}{n}} = (4.568 \cdot 10^{-14})^{\frac{1}{3.043}} = 4.134 \cdot 10^{-5}$$

$$\dot{Q}^{\frac{1}{n}} = (0.014286 * 10^{-6})^{\frac{1}{3.043}} = 2.643 \cdot 10^{-3}$$

Finally Δp_{square} from Eq. (6.1.2):

$$\Delta p_{\text{square}} = \frac{\dot{Q}^{\frac{1}{n}}}{K^{\frac{1}{n}} \cdot G} = \frac{2.643 \cdot 10^{-3}}{4.134 \cdot 10^{-5} * 1.956 \cdot 10^{-5}}$$

$$= 32.686 \text{ bar}$$

The above relationship for shear rate developed by RAMSTEINER [4] leads therefore almost to the same result as obtained in Method a.

Method c:

In this method first of all substitute radius is calculated from Eq. (6.1.14):

The pressure drop is then calculated using the same procedure as in the case of a round channel (Example 1):

Substitute radius R_{rh}:

$$R_{\text{rh}} = \left[\frac{\left(\frac{2^{n+1}}{\pi}\right) \cdot A^{n+2}}{B^{n+1}}\right]^{\frac{1}{n+3}}$$

$A = a^2 = 2.62^2 = 6.864 \text{ mm}^2$

$B = 4a = 4 * 2.62 = 10.48 \text{ mm}$

$n = 3.043$

$R_{\text{rh}} = 1.363 \text{ mm}$

Shear rate $\dot{\gamma}_a$ from Eq. (6.1.13):

$$\dot{\gamma}_a = \frac{4*0.014286}{\pi*0.1363} = 7.183 \text{ s}^{-1}$$

Viscosity η_a from Eq. (2.3.14):

$$\eta_a = 24\,205.54 * 7.183^{0.3286-1} = 6441.56 \text{ Pa} \cdot \text{s}$$

Shear stress τ from Eq. (2.3.4):

$$\tau = 46\,269.73 \text{ N/m}^2$$

Factor of proportionality from Eq. (2.3.8):

$$K = 4.568 \cdot 10^{-14}$$

G_{circle} from Eq. (6.1.3):

$$G_{\text{circle}} = \frac{\left(\frac{\pi}{4}\right)^{\frac{1}{3.043}} \cdot \left(\frac{1.363}{1000}\right)^{\frac{3}{3.043}+1}}{2*0.05}$$
$$= 1.885 \cdot 10^{-5}$$

Pressure drop from Eq. (6.1.2):

$$\Delta p = \frac{2.643 \cdot 10^{-3}}{4.134 \cdot 10^{-5} * 1.885 \cdot 10^{-5}} = 33.92 \text{ bar}$$

This result shows that the relationship, Eq. (6.1.14) [5] is sufficiently accurate for practical purposes. This equation is particularly useful for dimensioning channels, whose geometry differs from the common shape, namely, circle, slit or annulus. The procedure of calculation for an equilateral triangle is shown in the following example:

Example 6:

Melt flow through an equilateral triangular channel of length $L = 50$ mm. The side of the triangle $2d = 4.06$ mm. Other conditions remain the same as in Example 5.

Solution:

Substitute radius R_{rh} from Eq. (6.1.14) with

$$A = \sqrt{3} \cdot d^2 = 7.1376 \text{ mm}^2$$
$$B = 3*2d = 12.18 \text{ mm}$$

and

$$n = 3.043$$
$$R_{\text{rh}} = 1.274 \text{ mm}$$

Shear rate $\dot{\gamma}_a$ from Eq. (6.1.9):

$$\dot{\gamma}_a = \frac{4*0.014286}{\pi*0.1274^3} = 8.8 \text{ s}^{-1}$$

Viscosity η_a from Eq. (2.3.14):

$$\eta_a = 24\,205.54 * 8.8^{0.3286-1} = 5620.68 \text{ Pa}\cdot\text{s}$$

Shear stress τ from Eq. (2.3.4):

$$\tau = 49\,462 \text{ N/mm}^2$$

Factor of proportionality K from Eq. (2.3.8):

$$K = 4.568 \cdot 10^{-14}$$

G_{circle} from Eq. (6.1.3):

$$G_{\text{circle}} = \frac{\left(\dfrac{\pi}{4}\right)^{\frac{1}{3.043}} \cdot \left(\dfrac{1.274}{1000}\right)^{\frac{3}{3.043}+1}}{2*0.05}$$

$$= 1.648 \cdot 10^{-5}$$

Δp from Eq. (6.1.2):

$$\Delta p = \frac{\dot{Q}^{\frac{1}{n}}}{K^{\frac{1}{n}} \cdot G_{\text{circle}}}$$

$$= \frac{2.643 \cdot 10^{-3}}{4.134*10^{-5}*1.648*10^{-5}} = 38.79 \text{ bar}$$

Using the relation developed by RAMSTEINER [4] on the basis of rheological measurements on triangular channels Example 6 is calculated, as follows for the purpose of comparing both methods:

Shear rate from Eq. (6.1.12):

$$\dot{\gamma}_a = \frac{10}{3} \cdot \frac{\dot{Q}}{d^3}$$

$$= \frac{10}{3} * \frac{0.014286}{(2.03)^3} = 5.692 \text{ s}^{-1}$$

Viscosity η_a from Eq. (2.3.14):

$$\eta_a = 24\,205.54 * 5.692^{0.3286-1} = 7530.61 \text{ Pa}\cdot\text{s}$$

Shear stress τ from Eq. (2.3.4):

$$\tau = 42\,864.2 \text{ N/m}^2$$

Proportionality factor K from Eq. (2.3.8):

$$K = 4.568 \cdot 10^{-14}$$

Die constant $G_{triangle}$:

$$G_{triangle} = \frac{1}{\sqrt{3}} \cdot \left(\frac{3}{10}\right)^{\frac{1}{n}} \cdot \frac{d^{\frac{3}{n}+1}}{2L} \tag{6.1.17}$$

$$= \frac{1}{\sqrt{3}} \cdot \left(\frac{3}{10}\right)^{\frac{1}{3.043}} \cdot \frac{\left(\frac{2.03}{1000}\right)^{\frac{3}{3.043}+1}}{2*0.05} = 1.75 \cdot 10^{-5}$$

Pressure drop Δp from Eq. (6.1.2):

$$\Delta p = \frac{\dot{Q}^{\frac{1}{n}}}{K^{\frac{1}{n}} \cdot G_{triangle}}$$

$$= \frac{2.643 \cdot 10^{-3}}{4.134 \cdot 10^{-5} * 1.75 \cdot 10^{-5}} = 36.5 \text{ bar}$$

This result differs little from the one obtained by using the concept of substitute radius. Therefore this concept of SCHENKEL [5] is suitable for use in practice.

6.1.1.5   Temperature Rise and Residence Time

The adiabatic temperature increase of the melt can be calculated from

$$\Delta T = \frac{\Delta p}{10 \cdot \varrho_m \cdot c_{pm}} \text{ (K)} \tag{6.1.18}$$

where ΔT = temperature rise (K)
Δp = pressure difference (bar)
ϱ_m = melt density (g/cm^3)
c_{pm} = specific heat of the melt kJ/(kg·K)

The residence time $\bar{t}$ of the melt in the die of length L can be expressed as

$$\bar{t} = \frac{L}{\bar{u}} \tag{6.1.19}$$

$\bar{u}$ = average velocity of the melt

Eq. (6.1.19) for a tube can be written as

$$\bar{t} = \frac{4 \cdot L}{\dot{\gamma}_a R} \tag{6.1.20}$$

R = tube radius
$\dot{\gamma}_a$ = shear rate according to Eq. (6.1.9)

The relation for a slit is

$$\bar{t} = \frac{6 \cdot L}{H \dot{\gamma}_a} \tag{6.1.21}$$

H = height of slit
$\dot{\gamma}_a$ = shear rate from Eq. (6.1.10)

6.2 Extrusion Screws

In this chapter formulas for the quantities, which are often required to dimension extrusion screws and their use is illustrated by worked-out examples.

6.2.1 Solids Conveying

Under the assumptions that:
(a) the polymer moves through the screw channel as a plug
(b) there is no friction between the solid plastic and the screw and
(c) there is no pressure rise, the maximum flow rate $(\dot{Q}_s)_{max}$, Figs. 6.3 and 6.4 can be calculated from [6]

$$(\dot{Q}_s)_{max} = \pi^2 \cdot H \cdot D_b (D_b - H) \sin \phi \cos \phi * \frac{W}{W + w_{FLT}} \cdot N \tag{6.2.1}$$

The actual flow rate $\dot{Q}_s$ is given by [6]

$$\dot{Q}_s = \pi^2 \cdot H \cdot D_b (D_b - H) \cdot \frac{\tan \theta \cdot \tan \phi}{\tan \theta + \tan \phi} \cdot \frac{W}{W + w_{FLT}} \cdot N \tag{6.2.2}$$

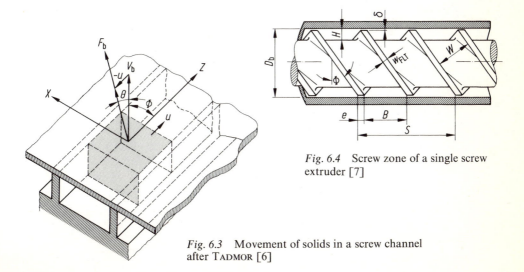

Fig. 6.4   Screw zone of a single screw extruder [7]

Fig. 6.3   Movement of solids in a screw channel after TADMOR [6]

The conveying efficiency η_F can be expressed as

$$\eta_F = \frac{\dot{Q}_s}{(\dot{Q}_s)_{max}} \tag{6.2.3}$$

In the practice this efficiency is also defined as

$$\eta_F = \frac{G_s}{N \cdot V_s \cdot \varrho_{os}} \tag{6.2.4}$$

where G_s = mass flow rate
$\quad\quad\;\; N$ = screw speed
$\quad\quad\;\; V_s$ = volume of the screw channel
$\quad\quad\;\; \varrho_{os}$ = bulk density

Example:

The geometry of the feed zone of a screw, Fig. (6.4), is given by the following data [6]:

barrel diameter $D_b = 50.57$ mm
screw lead $s = 50.57$ mm
number of flights $v = 1$
root diameter of the screw $D_s = 34.92$ mm
flight width $w_{FLT} = 5.057$ mm
depth of the feed zone $H = 7.823$ mm

The maximum specific flow rate and the actual flow rate are to be calculated.

Solution:

Helix angle ϕ:

$$\phi = \tan^{-1}\left(\frac{s}{\pi D_b}\right)$$

$$= \tan^{-1}\left(\frac{50.57}{\pi * 50.57}\right) = 17.66°$$

Width of the screw channel W:

$$W = \frac{s \cos \phi}{v} - w_{FLT}$$

$$= 50.57 * \cos 17.66 - 5.057$$

$$= 50.57 * 0.953 - 5.057 = 43.13 \text{ mm}$$

Maximum specific flow rate from Eq. (6.2.1):

$$\left(\frac{\dot{Q}_s}{N}\right)_{max} = \pi^2 * 0.7823 * 5.057 \cdot (5.057 - 0.7823)$$

$$*0.3034*0.953*\frac{4.313}{4.819}$$

$$=43.19 \text{ cm}^3/\text{rpm}$$

Taking the bulk density $\varrho_{os}=0.475$ g/cm^3 into account the specific mass flow rate becomes

$$\left(\frac{\dot{G}}{N}\right)_{max}=20.52 \text{ g/rpm}$$

The feed angle θ is required to calculate the actual flow rate. With the assumptions already made and assuming equal friction coefficients on screw f_s and barrel f_b the feed angle may be approximately calculated from [6]

$$\cos \theta = K \sin \theta + \sin \phi \left(K + \frac{D_s}{D_b} \cot \phi\right) \tag{6.2.5}$$

where

$$K = \frac{\bar{D}(\sin \phi + f_s \cos \phi)}{D_b(\cos \phi - f_b \sin \phi)} \tag{6.2.6}$$

With $f_s = f_b = 0.25$ and the average diameter $\bar{D}=D_b-H=5.057-0.7823=4.275$ cm

$$K = \frac{4.275(0.3034+0.25*0.953)}{5.057(0.953-0.25*0.3034)} = 0.522$$

With $K=0.522$ and $\dfrac{D_s}{D_b}=\dfrac{3.492}{5.057}=0.6906$ we obtain from Eq. (6.2.5)

$$\cos \theta = K \sin \theta + 0.816$$

$$\theta \approx 15.8°$$

Inserting $\theta=15.8°$ into Eq. (6.2.2)

$$\left(\frac{\dot{Q}_s}{N}\right)=\pi^2 \cdot H \cdot D_b(D_b-H)\cdot \frac{\tan \theta \cdot \tan \phi}{\tan \theta + \tan \phi}*\frac{W}{W+w_{FLT}}$$

gives

$$=\pi^2*0.7823*5.057(5.057-0.7823)$$

$$*\frac{\tan 15.8° \cdot \tan 17.66°}{\tan 15.8° + \tan 17.66}*\frac{4.313}{4.819}=22.4 \text{ cm}^3/\text{rpm}$$

The actual specific mass flow rate using the bulk density $\varrho_{os}=0.475$ g/cm^3 is therefore

$$\left(\frac{\dot{G}_s}{N}\right)=10.62 \text{ g/rpm}$$

The conveying efficiency η_F is

$$\eta_F=\frac{10.62}{20.52}=0.52$$

6.2.2   Melt Conveying

Starting from the parallel plate model and correcting it by means of appropriate correction factors [7] the throughput of melt in an extruder can be calculated. Although the following equation for the output applies to an isothermal quase-Newtonian fluid, it was found to be useful for many practical applications [3].

For a given geometry of the melt zone (Fig. 6.4) the output of a melt extruder or that of a melt pumping zone of a plasticating extruder can be determined as follows [7], [3]:

$$\text{Helix angle } \phi = \tan^{-1}\left[s/(\pi \cdot D_b)\right] \tag{6.2.7}$$

Volume flow rate of pressure flow $\dot{Q}_p$ (m³/s):

$$\dot{Q}_p = \frac{-\pi \cdot D_b \cdot H^3 \left(1 - \dfrac{v \cdot e}{s}\right) \cdot \sin^2 \phi \cdot \Delta p \cdot 10^{-4}}{12 \cdot \eta_a \cdot L} \tag{6.2.8}$$

Mass flow rate $\dot{m}_p$ (kg/h):

$$\dot{m}_p = 3600 \cdot 1000 \cdot \dot{Q}_p \cdot \varrho_m \tag{6.2.9}$$

Drag flow $\dot{Q}_d$ (m³/s):

$$\dot{Q}_d = \frac{\pi^2 \cdot D_b^2 \cdot N \cdot H \cdot \left(1 - \dfrac{v \cdot e}{s}\right) \cdot \sin \phi \cdot \cos \phi \cdot 10^{-9}}{2 * 60} \tag{6.2.10}$$

Mass flow rate $\dot{m}_d$ (kg/h):

$$\dot{m}_d = 3600 \cdot 1000 \cdot \dot{Q}_d \cdot \varrho_m \tag{6.2.11}$$

The leakage flow through the screw clearance is found from the ratios

$$a_d = -\frac{\dot{Q}_p}{\dot{Q}_d} \tag{6.2.12}$$

and

$$J = \frac{\delta}{H} \tag{6.1.13}$$

The extruder output $\dot{m}$ is finally calculated from

$$\dot{m} = 6 * 10^{-5} \cdot \pi^2 \cdot D_b^2 \cdot N \cdot H \cdot \left(1 - \frac{v \cdot e}{s}\right) * \varrho_m *$$

$$* \sin \phi \cdot \cos \phi \cdot (1 - a - J)/2 \tag{6.2.14}$$

The shear rate which is required for determining the viscosity η_a at the given melt temperature T is obtained from

$$\dot{\gamma}_a = \frac{\pi \cdot D_b \cdot N}{60 \cdot H} \tag{6.2.15}$$

Symbols and units used in the formulas above:

D_b:	Barrel diameter	mm
H:	Channel depth	mm
e:	Flight width	mm
s:	Screw lead	mm
δ:	Flight clearance	mm
L:	Length of melt zone	mm
v:	Number of flights	–
Δp:	Pressure difference across the melt zone	bar
$\dot{\gamma}_a$:	Shear rate	s^{-1}
$\dot{Q}_p, \dot{Q}_d$:	Volume flow rate of pressure flow and drag flow respectively	$\dfrac{m^3}{s}$
$\dot{m}_p, \dot{m}_d$:	Mass flow rate of pressure and drag flow respectively	kg/s
$\dot{m}$:	Extruder output	kg/h
η_a:	Melt viscosity	Pa·s
a_d:	Ratio of pressure flow to drag flow	–
T:	Melt temperature	°C
N:	Screw speed	min^{-1}

Example:

For the following conditions the extruder output is to be determined:

Resin: PE-LD with the same constants of viscosity as in Example 1 in Section 6.1.1.4

Process parameters:

Screw speed $N = 80$ min^{-1} (rpm)
Melt temperature $T = 200$ °C
Melt pressure $\Delta p = 300$ bar

Geometry of the metering zone:

$D_b = 60$ mm; $H = 3$ mm; $e = 6$ mm; $s = 60$ mm;
$\delta_{FLT} = 0.1$ mm; $L = 600$ mm; $v = 1$

Solution:

$\dot{\gamma}_a = 83.8$ s^{-1}	Eq. (6.2.15)
$a_T = 0.374$	Eq. (2.3.16)
$\eta_a = 1406.34$ Pa·s	Eq. (2.3.18)
$\varphi = 17.66°$	Eq. (6.2.7)
$\dot{m}_p = -3.146$ kg/h	Eqns. (6.2.8) and (6.2.9)
$\dot{m}_d = 46.42$ kg/h	Eqns. (6.2.10) and (6.2.11)
$\dot{m} = 41.8$ kg/h	Eqns. (6.2.12), (6.2.13) and (6.2.14)

Leakage flow $\dot{m}_1 = \dot{m}_d + \dot{m}_p - \dot{m} = 1.474$ kg/h.

6.2.2.1   Correction Factors

To correct the infinite parallel plate model for the flight edge effects following factors are to be used along with the equations given above:

With sufficient accuracy the shape factor for the drag flow F_d can be obtained from [8]

$$F_d = 1 - 0.571 \frac{H}{W} \tag{6.2.16}$$

and the factor for the pressure flow F_p

$$F_p = 1 - 0.625 \frac{H}{W} \tag{6.2.17}$$

The expressions for the corrected drag flow and pressure flow would be

$$\dot{Q}_{dk} = F_d \cdot \dot{Q}_d$$

and

$$\dot{Q}_{pk} = F_p \cdot \dot{Q}_p$$

The correction factor for the screw power which is treated in the next section can be determined from [9]

$$F_z = \exp(x) - x^3 + 2.2 x^2 - 1.05 x \tag{6.2.18}$$

with

$$x = \frac{H}{W}$$

Eq. (6.2.18) is valid in the range $0 < \dfrac{H}{W} < 2$. For the range of commonly occurring $\dfrac{H}{W}$-ratios in extruder screws the flight edge effect accounts for only less than 5% and can therefore be neglected [8]. The influence of screw curvature is also small so that F_x can be taken as 1.

Although the above mentioned factors are valid only for Newtonian fluids their use for polymer melt flow is justified.

6.2.2.2   Screw Power

The screw power consists of the power dissipated as viscous heat in the channel and flight clearance and the power required to raise the pressure of the melt. The total power Z_N is therefore for a melt filled zone [10]

$$Z_N = Z_c + Z_{FLT} + Z_{\Delta p} \tag{6.2.19}$$

where Z_c = power dissipated in the screw channel
Z_{FLT} = power dissipated in the flight clearance
$Z_{\Delta p}$ = power required to raise the pressure of the melt

The power dissipated in the screw channel Z_c is given by [10]

$$Z_c = \frac{v \cdot \pi^2 \cdot D_{FLT}^2 \cdot N^2 \cdot W \cdot \eta_c \cdot \Delta L (F_z \cos^2 \phi + 4 \sin^2 \phi)}{36 * 10^{14} \cdot \sin \phi \cdot H} \qquad (6.2.20)$$

The power dissipated in the flight clearance can be calculated from [10]

$$Z_{FLT} = \frac{v \cdot \pi^2 \cdot D_{FLT}^2 \cdot N^2 \cdot w_{FLT} \cdot \Delta L \cdot \eta_{FLT}}{36 * 10^{14} \cdot \delta_{FLT} \cdot \sin \phi} \qquad (6.2.21)$$

The power required to raise the pressure of the melt $Z_{\Delta p}$ can be written as

$$Z_{\Delta p} = 100 * \dot{Q}_p \cdot \Delta p \qquad (6.2.22)$$

The flight diameter D_{FLT} is obtained from

$$D_{FLT} = D_b - 2 \cdot \delta_{FLT} \qquad (6.2.23)$$

and the channel width W

$$W = \frac{s}{v} \cos \phi - w_{FLT} \qquad (6.2.24)$$

The symbols and units used in the equations above are given in the following example:

Example:

For the following conditions the screw power is to be determined:

Resin: PE-LD with the constants of viscosity as in Example 1 of Section 6.1.1.4

Operating conditions:
screw speed $N = 80$ rpm
melt temperature $T = 200$ °C
die pressure $\Delta p = 300$ bar

Geometry of the melt zone or metering zone:
$D_b = 60$ mm; $H = 3$ mm; $e = 6$ mm; $s = 60$ mm; $\delta_{FLT} = 0.1$ mm;
$\Delta L = 600$ mm; $v = 1$

Solution:

Power Z_c in the screw channel:

$$D_{FLT} = 59.8 \text{ mm from Eq. } (6.2.23)$$

Shear rate in the screw channel $\dot{\gamma}_c$:

$$\dot{\gamma}_c = 83.8 \text{ s}^{-1} \text{ from Eq. } (6.2.15)$$

$$a_T = 0.374 \text{ from Eq. } (2.3.16)$$

Viscosity of the melt in the screw channel η_c:

$$\eta_c = 1406.34 \text{ Pa} \cdot \text{s from Eq. } (2.3.18)$$

Channel width W:

$$W = 51.46 \text{ mm from Eq. (6.2.24)}$$

Number of flights v:

$$v = 1$$

Length of the melt zone ΔL:

$$\Delta L = 600 \text{ mm}$$

Factor F_x:

$$F_x = 1 \text{ for } \frac{H}{W} = \frac{3}{51.46} = 0.058 \text{ from Eq. (6.2.18)}$$

Helix angle ϕ:

$$\phi = 17.66°; \quad \sin \phi = 0.303 \text{ from Eq. (6.2.7)}$$

Power in the screw channel Z_c from Eq. (6.2.20):

$$Z_c = 1 * \pi^2 * 59.8^2 * 80^2 * 51.46 * 1406.34 * 600 *$$

$$* \frac{(1 \cdot \cos^2 17.66° + 4 \sin^2 17.66°)}{36 \cdot 10^{14} * 3 * \sin 17.66°} = 3.84 \text{ kW}$$

Power in the flight clearance Z_{FLT}:

Flight width W_{FLT} (Fig. 6.4):

$$w_{FLT} = e \cos \phi = 6 * \cos 17.66° = 5.7 \text{ mm}$$

Shear rate in the flight clearance $\dot{\gamma}_{FLT}$:

$$\dot{\gamma}_{FLT} = \frac{\pi \cdot D_b \cdot N}{60 \cdot \delta_{FLT}} = \frac{\pi * 60 * 80}{60 * 0.1} = 2513.3 \text{ s}^{-1}$$

Shift factor a_T:

$$a_T = 0.374 \text{ at } T = 200 \text{ °C from Eq. (2.3.16)}$$

Viscosity in the flight clearance η_{FLT}:

$$\eta_{FLT} = 219.7 \text{ Pa} \cdot \text{s from Eq. (2.3.18)}$$

Length of the melt zone ΔL:

$$\Delta L = 600 \text{ mm}$$

Z_{FLT} from Eq. (6.2.21).

$$Z_{FLT} = \frac{1 * \pi^2 * 59.8^2 * 80^2 * 600 * 5.7 * 219.7}{36 * 10^{14} * 0.1 * 0.303} = 1.56 \text{ kW}$$

Power to raise the melt pressure $Z_{\Delta p}$:

Pressure flow $\dot{Q}_p$:

$\dot{Q}_p$ from the Example in Section 6.2.2

$$\dot{Q}_p = 1.249 * 10^{-6}\, \text{m}^3/\text{s}$$

Die pressure Δp:

$$\Delta p = 300 \text{ bar}$$

$Z_{\Delta p}$ from Eq. (6.2.22):

$$Z_{\Delta p} = 100 * 1.249 * 10^{-6} * 300$$
$$= 0.0375 \text{ kW}$$

Hence the power $Z_{\Delta p}$ is negligible in comparison with the sum $Z_c + Z_{FLT}$.

6.2.2.3 Heat Transfer between the Melt and the Barrel

To estimate the power required to heat the barrel or to calculate the heat lost from the melt the heat transfer coefficient of the melt at the barrel wall is needed. This can be estimated from [11]

$$\alpha_{sz} = \lambda_m \left(\frac{N}{60 \cdot \pi \cdot a}\right)^{0.5} \left[1 - \frac{(T_f - T_m)\{1 - \exp(\beta)\}}{(T_b - T_m)}\right] \tag{6.2.25}$$

where the thermal diffusivity a

$$a = \frac{\lambda_m}{10^6 \cdot c_{pm} \cdot \varrho_m} \tag{6.2.26}$$

and the parameter β

$$\beta = -\frac{10^{-6} \cdot \delta_{FLT}^2 \cdot N}{240 * a} \tag{6.2.27}$$

Indices:

m: melt
f: melt film
b: barrel

Example with symbols and units:

Thermal conductivity $\lambda_m = 0.174\, \dfrac{\text{W}}{\text{m} \cdot \text{K}}$

Specific heat $\qquad c_{pm} = 2\, \dfrac{\text{kJ}}{\text{kg} \cdot \text{K}}$

Melt density $\qquad \varrho_m = 0.7 \text{ g/cm}^3$

Thermal diffusivity a from Eq. (6.2.26):

$$a = 1.243 * 10^{-7} \, m^2/s$$

Flight clearance $\delta_{FLT} = 0.1$ mm

Screw speed $N = 80$ rpm

Parameter β from Eq. (6.2.27):

$$\beta = -0.027$$

For $T_f = 137.74\,°C$, $T_m = 110\,°C$ and $T_b = 150\,°C$

α_{sz} from Eq. (6.2.25):

$$\alpha_{sz} = 0.174 \left(\frac{80 * 10^7}{60 \cdot \pi \cdot 1.243} \right)^{0.5} \left[1 - \frac{(137.7 - 110)\{1 - \exp(-0.027)\}}{(150 - 110)} \right]$$

$$\alpha_{sz} = 315.5 \, W/(m^2 \cdot K)$$

6.2.2.4   Melt temperature

The exact calculation of melt or stock temperature can be done only on an iterative basis as shown in the computer program given in [9]. The following relationships and the numerical example illustrate the basis of calculating the stock temperature. The result obtained can only be an estimate of the real value, as exact iteration lacks.

Temperature rise ΔT:

$$\Delta T = (T_{out} - T_M) = \frac{3600(Z_c + Z_{FLT} + N_H)}{\dot{m} \cdot C_{pm}} \tag{6.2.28}$$

Heat through the barrel or heat lost from the melt:

$$N_H = \frac{\alpha_{sz} \cdot \pi \cdot D_{FLT} \cdot \Delta L (T_b - T_{EIN})}{10^6 \cdot \cos \phi} \tag{6.2.29}$$

Example for calculating N_H with symbols and units:

$\alpha_s = 315.5 \, W/(m^2 \cdot K)$; $D_{FLT} = 59$ mm; $\Delta L = 600$ nm;
$T_b = 150\,°C$; $c_{pm} = 2 \, kJ/(kg \cdot K)$

Stock temperature at the inlet of the screw increment considered:

$$T_{in} = 200\,°C$$

N_H from Eq. (6.2.29):

$$N_H = \frac{315.5 * \pi * 59.8 * 600 * 50}{10^6 * \cos 17.66°}$$

$$= -1.86 \, kW \text{ (heat loss from the melt)}$$

ΔT with the values $Z_c = 3.84$ kW, $Z_{FLT} = 1.56$ kW and $\dot{m} = 41.8$ kg/h from the earlier example from Eq. (6.2.28)

$$\Delta T = \frac{3600 * 3.54}{41.8 * 2} = 152.4 \text{ °C}$$

Stock temperature at the outlet of the screw increment considered T_{out}:

$$T_{out} = T_M + 152.4 \text{ °C}$$

Melting point of the polymer $T_M = 110$ °C

Hence $T_{out} = 110 + 152.4 = 262.4$ °C

Average stock temperature $\bar{T}$:

$$\bar{T} = \frac{T_{in} + T_{out}}{2} = \frac{200 + 262.4}{2} = 231.2 \text{ °C}$$

As already mentioned this result can only be an estimate because the effect of the change of temperature on the viscosity can be calculated only through an iterative procedure as shown in [9].

6.2.2.5   Melt Pressure

For a screw zone of constant depth the melt or stock pressure can be obtained generally from the pressure flow by means of Eq. (6.2.8). However, the following empirical equation [10] has been found to give good results in the practice:

$$|\Delta p| = \frac{F_1 \cdot 2 \cdot \eta_p \cdot \Delta l}{\sin \phi (H_{out} + \delta_{FLT})}$$
$$* \left[\frac{|\dot{Q}_p| (2 n_R + 1) \cdot (H_R + H_R^2) \cdot 10^9}{W (H_{out} + \delta_f)^2 \cdot n_R \cdot v} \right]^{n_R} \cdot 10^{-5} \qquad (6.2.30)$$

where

$$\eta_p = \frac{\eta_\alpha}{\dot{\gamma}^{n_R - 1}} \qquad (6.2.31)$$

The sign of Δp corresponds to that of the pressure flow $\dot{Q}_p$.

Example with symbols and units:

a) Screw zone of constant channel depth (metering zone)

Empirical factor	$F_1 = 0.286$
Melt viscosity in screw channel	$\eta_\alpha = 1400$ Pa·s
Shear rate in channel	$\dot{\gamma} = 84$ s^{-1}
Length of screw zone (or of an increment)	$\Delta l = 600$ mm
Helix angle	$\phi = 17.66°$

Channel depth at the outlet of the zone or increment $H_{out}=3$ mm
Flight clearance $\delta_{FLT}=0.1$ mm
Pressure flow $\dot{Q}_p=1.249\cdot10^{-6}$ m^3/s
Reciprocal of the power law exponent n $n_R=0.5$
Ratio of channel depths at the outlet (H_{out}) and
  inlet (H_{in}) of the zone or increment H_R $H_R=1$ (constant depth)
Width of the channel $W=51.46$ mm
Thickness of the melt film $\delta_f=0$
Number of flights $v=1$

η_p from Eq. (6.2.31):

$$\eta_p=\frac{1400}{84^{0.5-1}}=12831$$

Δp from Eq. (6.2.30):

$$\Delta p=\left\{\frac{0.286*2*600*12831}{\sin 17.66°(3+0.1)}\right\}$$
$$\cdot\left[1.249*10^{-6}(2*0.5+1)*\frac{(1+1)*10^9}{51.46*3^2*0.5*1}\right]^{0.5}\cdot10^{-5}$$
$$=218\text{ bar}$$

b) *Screw zone of varying depth (transition zone)*

$H_{in}=9$ mm; $H_{out}=3$ mm; $\Delta l=240$ mm; $\eta=1800$ Pa$\cdot$s; $\dot{\gamma}=42$ s^{-1}

η_p from Eq. (6.2.31):

$$\eta_p=\frac{1800}{42^{0.5-1}}=11665$$

Δp from (6.2.30):

$$\Delta p=\frac{0.286*2*240*11665}{\sin 17.66°*3.1}$$
$$\cdot\left[1.249*10^{-6}*\left\{\left(\frac{3}{9}\right)+\left(\frac{3}{9}\right)^2\right\}*\frac{10^9}{51.46*3^2*0.5}\right]^{0.5}\cdot10^{-5}$$
$$=37.2\text{ bar}$$

The more exact calculation of the melt pressure profile in an extruder should consider the effect of the ratio of pressure flow to drag flow, the so-called drossel quotient, as shown in [10].

6.2.3 Melting of Solids

Physical models describing the melting of solids in extruder channels were developed by many workers, notable among them being the work of TADMOR [6]. RAUWENDAAL summarises the theories underlying these models in his book [8]. Detailed computer programs for calculating melting profiles which are based on these models, have been given by RAO in his books [3], [9].

The purpose of the following section is to illustrate the calculation of the main parameters occurring in these models through numerical examples. The important steps for obtaining a melting profile are treated in an another section for a quasi Newtonian fluid.

6.2.3.1 Thickness of Melt Film

According to the Tadmor model [6] the maximum thickness of the melt film (Fig. 6.5) is given by

$$\delta_{max} = \left\{ \frac{[2\lambda_m(T_b - T_m) + \eta_f \, V_j^2 \cdot 10^{-4}] \, W}{10^3 \cdot V_{bx} \cdot \varrho_m \, [c_{ps}(T_m - T_s) + i_m]} \right\}^{0.5} \tag{6.2.32}$$

Example with symbols and units:

Thermal conductivity of the melt	$\lambda_m = 0.174 \dfrac{W}{mK}$
Barrel temperature	$T_b = 150\ ^\circ C$
Melting point of the polymer	$T_m = 110\ ^\circ C$
Viscosity in the melt film	$\eta_f\ Pa \cdot s$
Shear rate in the film	$\dot{\gamma}_f\ s^{-1}$
Velocity of the barrel surface	$V_b\ cm/s$
Velocity components V_{bx}, V_{bz}	cm/s (Fig. 6.6)
Velocity of the solid bed	$V_{sz}\ cm/s$
Output of the extruder	$G = 16.67\ g/s$
Average film thickness	$\bar{\delta}_f\ mm$
Temperature of the melt in the film	$\bar{T}_f\ ^\circ C$
Average film temperature	$T_a\ ^\circ C$
Depth of the feed zone	$H_1 = 9\ mm$
Width of the screw channel	$W = 51.46\ mm$
Melt density	$\varrho_m = 0.7\ g/cm^3$
Density of the solid polymer	$\varrho_s = 0.92\ g/cm^3$
Specific heat of the solid polymer	$c_{ps} = 2.2\ kJ/(kg \cdot K)$
Temperature of the solid polymer	$T_s = 20\ ^\circ C$
Heat of fusion of the polymer	$i_m = 125.5\ kJ/kg$
Maximum film thickness	$\delta_{max}\ cm$

Indices:

m: melt; s: solid

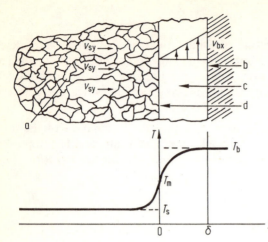

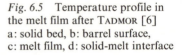

Fig. 6.5   Temperature profile in the melt film after TADMOR [6] a: solid bed, b: barrel surface, c: melt film, d: solid-melt interface

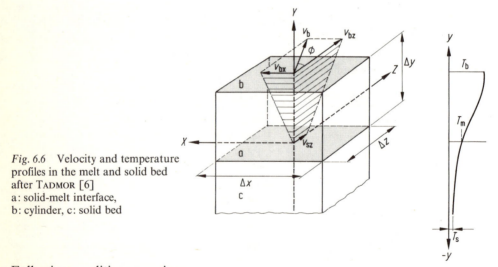

Fig. 6.6   Velocity and temperature profiles in the melt and solid bed after TADMOR [6] a: solid-melt interface, b: cylinder, c: solid bed

Following conditions are given:

The resin is PE-LD with the same constants of viscosity as in Example 1 of Section 6.1.1.4.

The barrel diameter D_b is 60 mm and the screw speed is 80 rpm.

$$V_b = \frac{\pi \cdot D_b \cdot N}{10 * 60} = \frac{\pi \cdot 60 \cdot 80}{10 * 60} = 25.13 \text{ cm/s}$$

$$V_{bx} = V_b \sin \phi = 25.1 * \sin 17.66° = 7.62 \text{ cm/s}$$

$$V_{bz} = V_b \cdot \cos \phi = 25.1 * \cos 17.66° = 23.95 \text{ cm/s}$$

$$V_{sz} = \frac{100 \cdot G}{W \cdot H_1 \cdot \varrho_s} = \frac{100 * 16.67}{51.46 * 9 * 0.92} = 3.91 \text{ cm/s}$$

Relative velocity V_j (Fig. 6.6):

$$V_j = (V_b^2 + V_{sz}^2 - 2V_b \cdot V_{sz} \cdot \cos\phi)^{0.5}$$
$$= (25.13^2 + 3.91^2 - 2*25.13*3.91*\cos 17.66°)^{0.5}$$
$$= 21.44 \text{ cm/s}$$

Temperature $\bar{T}_a$:

$$\bar{T}_a = \frac{T_b + T_m}{2} = \frac{150 + 110}{2} = 130 \text{ °C}$$

$$\dot{\gamma}_a = \frac{V_j}{\delta_f}$$

Starting from an assumed film thickness of 0.1 mm and using the temperature resulting when heat generation is neglected, the viscosity in the film is first estimated. By changing then the film thickness and repeating this calculation the final viscosity is obtained [3].

This iteration leads to

$$\dot{\gamma}_f = \frac{V_j}{\delta_f} = \frac{2*21.44*10}{0.299} = 1434 \text{ s}^{-1}$$

$$\eta_f = 351.84 \text{ Pa·s}$$

δ_{max} from Eq. (6.2.32):

$$\delta_{max} = \Big\{ [2*0.174(150 - 110) + 351.84*21.44^2*10^{-4}]$$
$$* \frac{51.46}{10^3*7.62*0.7[2.2(110-20)+125.5]} \Big\}^{0.5}$$
$$= 0.0299 \text{ cm, or } 0.299 \text{ mm}$$

6.2.3.1.1 Temperature in Melt Film

Taking the viscous heat generation into account the temperature in melt film can be obtained from [6]

$$\bar{T}_f = \bar{T}_a + \frac{10^{-4} \cdot \eta_f \cdot V_j^2}{12 \cdot \lambda_m} \tag{6.2.33}$$

$$\bar{T}_f - \bar{T}_a = \frac{10^{-4}*351.84*21.44^2}{12*0.174} = 7.75 \text{ °C}$$

$$\bar{T}_f = \left(\frac{150+110}{2}\right) + 7.75 = 137.75 \text{ °C}$$

As seen from the equations above the desired quantities have to be calculated on an iterative basis. This is done by the computer program given in [3].

6.2.3.2   Melting Rate

The melting rate is described by TADMOR [6] through the parameter ϕ_p, which is expressed as

$$\phi_p = \left\{ \frac{V_{bx} \cdot \varrho_m \cdot [\lambda_m(T_b - T_m) + 0.5\,\eta_f \cdot V_j^2 \cdot 10^{-4}]}{100 * 2[c_{ps}(T_m - T_s) + i_m]} \right\}^{0.5} \qquad (6.2.34)$$

The numerator represents the heat supplied to the polymer by conduction through the barrel and dissipation, where as the denominator shows the enthalpy required to melt the solid polymer. The melting rate increases with increasing ϕ_p.

By inserting the values given above into Eq. (6.2.34) we obtain

$$\phi_p = \left\{ \frac{7.62 * 0.7\,[0.174(150 - 110) + 0.5 * 351.84 * 21.44^2 * 10^{-4}]}{100 * 2\,[2.2(110 - 20) + 125.5]} \right\}^{0.5}$$

$$= 0.035 \,\frac{\text{g}}{\text{cm}^{1.5}\,\text{s}}$$

6.2.3.3   Dimensionless Melting Parameter

The dimensionless melting parameter ψ is defined as [6]

$$\psi = \frac{\phi_p \cdot H_1 \cdot W^{0.5}}{10^{1.5} \cdot G} \qquad (6.2.35)$$

with $\phi_p = 0.035$ g/(cm$^{1.5}$·s)
$\quad H_1 = 9$ mm
$\quad W = 51.46$ mm and
$\quad G = 16.67$ g/s

we get
$\quad \psi = 0.004$

The dimensionless parameter is the ratio between the amount of melted polymer per unit down channel distance to the extruder output per unit channel feed depth.

6.2.3.4   Melting Profile

The melting profile gives the amount of unmelted polymer as a function of screw length (Fig. 6.7) and is the basis for calculating the stock temperature and pressure. It thus shows whether the polymer at the end of the screw is fully melted. As is known, the plasticating and mixing capacity of a screw can be improved by mixing devices. Knowledge of the melting profile enables to judge the suitable positioning of mixing and shearing devices in the screw [21].

The following equation applies to a screw zone of constant depth [6]

$$\frac{X_{out}}{W} = \frac{X_{in}}{W} \left(1 - \frac{\psi \cdot \Delta z}{2H_1} \right)^2 \qquad (6.2.36)$$

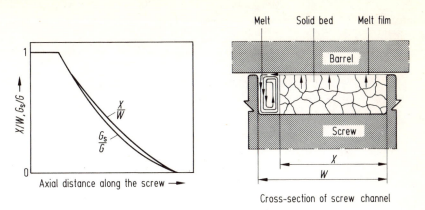

Fig. 6.7   Solid bed or melting profiles X/W and G_s/G [21]
G: total mass flow rate, G_s: mass flow rate of solids

and for a tapered channel [6]

$$\frac{X_{out}}{W} = \frac{X_{in}}{W}\left[\frac{\psi}{A} - \left(\frac{\psi}{A} - 1\right)\sqrt{\frac{H_{in}}{H_{out}}}\right]^2 \tag{6.2.37}$$

where

$$A = \frac{H_1 - H_2}{Z} \tag{6.2.38}$$

The parameter ψ is obtained from Eq. (6.2.35).

Symbols and units:

X_{out}, X_{in}	mm	Width of the solid bed at the outlet and inlet of a screw increment respectively
W	mm	Channel width
ψ		Melting parameter
Δz	mm	Downchannel distance of the increment
H_{in}, H_{out}	mm	Channel depth at the inlet and outlet of an increment
H_1, H_2	mm	Channel depth of a parallel zone (feed zone) and depth at the end of a transition zone (Fig. 6.8)
A		Relative decrease of channel depth, Eq. (6.2.38)
Z	mm	Downchannel length of a screw zone

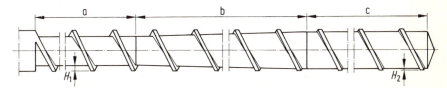

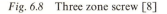

Fig. 6.8   Three zone screw [8]

Example:

a) Constant channel depth

For

$H_1 = 9$ mm; $X_{in}/W = 1$; $\Delta z = 99$ mm and $\psi = 0.004$ from Section 6.2.3.3, X_{out}/W can be calculated from Eq. (6.2.36):

$$\frac{X_{out}}{W} = 1\left(1 - \frac{0.004 * 99}{2 * 9}\right)^2 = 0.96$$

This means that at a distance of $\Delta z = 99$ mm 4 per cent of the solids were melted.

b) Varying channel depth

For the values

$$H_1 = 9 \text{ mm}$$
$$H_2 = 3 \text{ mm}$$
$$Z = 1584 \text{ mm}$$
$$X_{in}/W = 0.96$$
$$H_{in} = 9 \text{ mm}$$
$$H_{out} = 8.625$$

ψ can be obtained from Eq. (6.2.35):

$$\psi = \frac{\phi_p \cdot H_1 \cdot \sqrt{W}}{10^{1.5} \cdot \left(\frac{X_{in}}{W}\right) \cdot G} = \frac{0.035 * 9 * \sqrt{51.46}}{10^{1.5} * 0.96 * 16.67} = 0.00447$$

The relative decrease of the channel depth A is calculated from Eq. (6.2.38):

$$A = \frac{H_1 - H_2}{Z} = \frac{(9-3)}{1584} = 0.00379$$

and $\dfrac{X_{out}}{W}$ from Eq. (6.2.37)

$$\frac{X_{out}}{W} = 0.96\left[\frac{0.00447}{0.00379} - \left(\frac{0.00447}{0.00379} - 1\right)\sqrt{\frac{9}{8.625}}\right]^2 = 0.953$$

Assuming a constant velocity of the solid bed the mass flow ratio G_s/G results from

$$\frac{G_s}{G} = \frac{\bar{X}\bar{H}}{WH_1} \qquad\qquad (6.2.39)$$

where G_s = mass flow rate of the solid polymer g/s
$\quad\quad\quad$ G = throughout of the extruder g/s
$\quad\quad\quad$ $\bar{X}$ = average of X_{in} and X_{out} mm
$\quad\quad\quad$ $\bar{H}$ = average of H_{out} and H_{in} mm

For a zone of constant depth it follows that

$$\frac{G_s}{G} = \frac{\bar{X}}{W}$$

(6.2.40)

a) Constant depth:

$$\frac{\bar{X}}{W} = 0.5 \left(\frac{X_{in}}{W} + \frac{X_{out}}{W} \right) = 0.5 * 1.96 = 0.98$$

$$\frac{G_s}{G} = 0.98$$

b) Varying depth:

$$\frac{\bar{X}}{W} = 0.5 \left(\frac{X_{in}}{W} + \frac{X_{out}}{W} \right) = 0.5 (0.96 + 0.953) = 0.9565$$

$$\frac{\bar{H}}{H_1} = 0.5 \left(\frac{H_{in}}{H_1} + \frac{H_{out}}{H_1} \right) = 0.5 \left(\frac{9}{9} + \frac{8.625}{9} \right) = 0.9792$$

$$\frac{G_s}{G} = \frac{\bar{X}}{W} \cdot \frac{\bar{H}}{H_1} = 0.9366$$

The profiles of stock temperature and pressure can be calculated from the melting profile by using the width of the melt filled part of the channel in the equations given in Section 6.2.2 [10].

6.2.4   Temperature Fluctuation of Melt

Temperature and pressure variations of the melt in an extruder serve as a measure for the quality of the extrudate and provide information as to the performance of the screw.

The temperature variation ΔT may be estimated from the following empirical relation, which was developed from the results of experiments of SQUIRES [12] conducted on 3-Zone screws:

$$\Delta T = \frac{5}{9} \left[\frac{1}{4.31 \, N_Q^2 - 0.024} \right]$$

(6.2.41)

This relation is valid for $0.11 < N_Q < 0.5$.

The parameter N_Q is given by

$$N_Q = 14.7 \cdot 10^{-4} \frac{D_b^2}{G} \sum \frac{L}{H}$$

(6.2.42)

where ΔT = temperature variation   °C
$\quad\quad\quad D_b$ = barrel diameter   cm

G = extruder output   g/s
L = length of screw zone in diameters
H = depth of the screw zone   cm

Example:

Following values are given:

$D_b = 6$ cm
$G = 15$ g/s

L	depth cm	L/H
9	0.9	10
3	0.6 (mean value)	3.33
9	0.3	30

Hence $\Sigma \dfrac{L}{H} = 43.33$

N_Q from Eq. (6.2.42):

$$N_Q = 14.7 * 10^{-4} * \frac{36}{15} * 43.33 = 0.153$$

ΔT from Eq. (6.2.41):

$$\Delta T = \frac{5}{9}\left[\frac{1}{4.31 * 0.153^2 - 0.024}\right] = 7.22 \,°C \text{ or } \pm 3.61 \,°C$$

The constants occurring in the Eqs. (6.2.41) and (6.2.42) depend on the type of polymer used. For screws other than 3-Zone screws the geometry term in Eq. (6.2.42) has to be defined in such a way that N_Q correlates well with the measured temperature fluctuations.

6.2.5   Scale-up of Screw Extruders

Based on the laws of similarity PEARSON [13] developed a set of relationships to scale up a single screw extruder. These relations are useful for the practising engineer to estimate the size of a larger extruder from experimental data gathered on a smaller machine. The scale-up assumes equal length to diameter ratios between the two extruders. The important relations can be summarised as follows:

$$\frac{H_2}{H_1} = \left(\frac{D_2}{D_1}\right)^{(1-s)/(2-3s)} \tag{6.2.43}$$

$$\frac{N_2}{N_1} = \left(\frac{D_2}{D_1}\right)^{-(2-2s)/(2-3s)} \tag{6.2.44}$$

$$\frac{\dot{m}_2}{\dot{m}_1} = \left(\frac{D_2}{D_1}\right)^{(3-5s)/(2-3s)} \tag{6.2.45}$$

$$\frac{H_{F_2}}{H_{F_1}} = \left(\frac{D_2}{D_1}\right)^{(1-s)/(2-3s)}$$

(6.2.46)

where H_F = feed depth
H = metering depth
D = screw diameter
N = screw speed

Indices: 1, 2 = screw of known geometry and screw, the geometry of which is to be determined respectively.

The exponent s is given by

$$s = 0.5\,(1 - n_R)$$

where n_R is the reciprocal of the power law exponent n. The shear rate required to determine n is obtained from

$$\dot{\gamma}_a = \frac{\pi \cdot D_1 \cdot N_1}{60 \cdot H_1}$$

Example:

Following conditions are given:

The resin is PE-LD with the same constants of viscosity as in Example 1 of Section 6.1.1.4. The stock temperature is 200 °C. The data pertaining to screw 1 are:

$D_1 = 90$ mm; $H_F = 12$ mm; $H_1 = 4$ mm

feed length   = 9 D_1
transition length = 2 D_1
metering length = 9 D_1
output $\dot{m}_1$ = 130 kg/h
screw speed N_1 = 80 rpm

The diameter of screw 2 is $D_2 = 120$ mm. The geometry of screw 2 is to be determined.

Solution:

The geometry is computed from the equations given above [3]. It follows that

$D_2 = 120$ mm
$H_{F_2} = 14.41$ mm
$H_2 = 4.8$ mm
$\dot{m}_2 = 192.5$ kg/h
$N_2 = 55.5$ rpm

Other methods of scaling-up have been treated by SCHENKEL [29], FENNER [30], FISCHER [31] and POTENTE [32].

6.2.6   Mechanical Design of Extrusion Screws

6.2.6.1   Torsion

The maximum shear stress τ_{max}, which occurs at the circumference of the screw root as a result of the torque M_T is given by [8]

$$\tau_{max} = \frac{2 \cdot M_T}{\pi \cdot R^3} \tag{6.2.47}$$

where R = root radius of the screw

The maximum feed depth H_{max} can be computed from [8]

$$H_{max} = 0.5 D - \left(\frac{2 \cdot M_T}{\pi \tau_{zul}}\right)^{\frac{1}{3}} \tag{6.2.48}$$

where D = diameter
τ_{zul} = allowable shear stress of the screw metal

Example [8]:

The maximum feed depth is to be calculated for the following conditions:

$D = 150$ mm; $M_T = 17810$ Nm; $\tau_{zul} = 100$ MPa;
H_{max} is found from Eq. (6.2.48):

$$H_{max} = \frac{1}{2} * \frac{150}{1000} - \left(\frac{2 * 17810}{\pi * 100 * 10^6}\right)^{\frac{1}{3}}$$

$$= 0.075 - 0.0485 = 0.0265 \text{ m} \quad \text{or} \quad 26.5 \text{ mm.}$$

6.2.6.2   Deflection

6.2.6.2.1   Lateral Deflection

The lateral deflection of the screw (Fig. 6.9) caused by its own weight can be obtained from [8]

$$Y(L) = \frac{2 * 1000 \cdot g \cdot \varrho \cdot L^4}{E \cdot D^2} \tag{6.2.49}$$

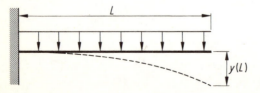

Fig. 6.9   Lateral deflection of the screw as cantilever [8]

Numerical example with symbols and units [8]:

$g = 9.81 \text{ m}^2/\text{s}$ acceleration due to gravity
$\varrho = 7850 \text{ kg/m}^3$ density of the screw metal
$L = 3 \text{ m}$ length of the screw
$E = 210 * 10^9 \text{ Pa}$ elastic modulus of the screw metal
$D = 0.15 \text{ m}$ screw diameter

Inserting these values into Eq. (6.2.49) we get

$$Y(L) = \frac{2 * 1000 * 9.81 * 7850 * 3^4}{210 * 10^9 * 0.15 * 0.15}$$

$$= 2.64 \text{ mm}$$

This value exceeds the usual flight clearance, so that the melt between the screw and the barrel takes on the role of supporting the screw to prevent contact between the screw and the barrel [8].

6.2.6.2.2 Buckling Due to Die Pressure

The critical die pressure which can cause buckling can be calculated from [8]

$$P_{\text{K}} = \frac{10^{-5} \cdot \pi^2 \cdot E}{64 \cdot \left(\dfrac{L}{D}\right)^2} \tag{6.2.50}$$

Numerical example [8]:

$E = 210 * 10^9 \text{ Pa}$ elastic modulus of the screw metal
$L/D = 35$ length to diameter ratio of screw

P_{K} from Eq. (6.2.50):

$$P_{\text{K}} = \frac{10^{-5} * \pi^2 * 210 * 10^9}{64 * 35^2} = 264.36 \text{ bar}$$

As can be seen from Eq. (6.2.50), the critical die pressure P_{K} decreases with increasing ratio L/D. This means, that for the usual range of die pressures 200–600 bar buckling through die pressure is a possibility, when the ratio L/D is greater than 20 [8].

6.2.6.2.3 Screw Vibration

When the screw speed corresponds to the natural frequency of lateral vibration of the shaft, the resulting resonance leads to large amplitudes, which can cause screw deflection.

The critical screw speed according to [8] is given by

$$N_{\text{k}} = 0.88 \frac{D}{L^2} \left(\frac{E}{\varrho}\right)^{\frac{1}{2}} \tag{6.2.51}$$

Substituting the values for steel, $E = 210 * 10^9$ Pa and $\varrho = 7850$ kg/m^3 we get

$$N_k = \frac{4549.5}{D \cdot \left(\dfrac{L}{D}\right)^2} \qquad\qquad (6.2.52)$$

Numerical example:

For $D = 150$ mm and $\dfrac{L}{D} = 30$, N_R is found from Eq. (6.2.52)

$$N_k = \frac{4549.5}{0.15 * 30^2} = 33.7 \text{ ups or } 2022 \text{ upm}$$

This result shows, that at the normal range of screw speeds vibrations due to resonance are unlikely.

6.2.6.2.4   Uneven Distribution of Pressure

The non-uniform pressure distribution around the circumference of the screw can lead to vertical and horizontal forces of such a magnitude, that the screw deflects into the barrel. Even a pressure difference of 10 bar could create a horizontal force F_h in an extruder of $D = 150$ mm within a section of length $L = 150$ mm

$$F_h = \Delta p \cdot D \cdot L = 10 * 10^5 * 0.15 * 0.15 = 22.5 \text{ kN}$$

According to RAUWENDAAL [8] the non-uniform pressure distribution is the most probable cause of screw deflection.

6.3   Injection Molding

Compared to extrusion, injection molding runs discontinously and therefore the stages involved in this process are time-dependent [14]. The quantitative description of the important mold filling stage has been made possible by the well-known computer programs like MOLDFLOW [15] and CADMOULD [16]. The purpose of this section is to present the basic formulas necessary for designing the injection molding dies and screws on a rheological and thermal basis and illustrate the use of these formulas with examples.

6.3.1   Pressure Drop in Runner

As the following example shows, the pressure drop along the runner of an injection mold can be calculated from the same relationships used for dimensioning extrusion dies.

Example:

For the following data the isothermal pressure drop Δp_0 and the adiabatic pressure drop Δp are to be determined:

The resin is a polystyrene with the viscosity constants according to Eq. (2.3.18), Section 2.3.7.3:

$A_0 = 4.4475$
$A_1 = -0.4983$
$A_2 = -0.1743$
$A_3 = 0.03594$
$A_4 = -0.002196$
$c_1 = 4.285$
$c_2 = 133.2$
$T_0 = 190\,°C$

flow rate	$\dot{m} = 330.4$ kg/h
melt density	$\varrho_m = 1.12$ g/cm^3
specific heat	$c_{pm} = 1.6$ kJ/(kg·K)
melt temperature	$T = 230\,°C$
length of the runner	$L = 101.6$ mm
radius of the runner	$R = 5.08$ mm

Solution:

a) Isothermal flow

$\dot{\gamma}_a$ from Eq. (2.3.1):

$$\dot{\gamma}_a = \frac{4\dot{Q}}{\pi R^3} = \frac{4*330.4}{3.6*\pi*1.12*(0.508)^3}$$

$$= 795.8 \text{ s}^{-1}$$

($\dot{Q}$ = volume flow rate cm^3/s)

a_T from Eq. (2.3.17):

$$a_T = 10^{\frac{-c_1(T-T_0)}{c_2+(T-T_0)}}$$

$$= 10^{\frac{-4.285(230-190)}{133.2+(230-190)}} = 10^{-0.9896} = 0.102$$

n from Eq. (2.3.19):

$$n = 5.956$$

η_a from Eq. (2.3.18):

$$\eta_a = 132 \text{ Pa·s}$$

τ from Eq. (2.3.4):

$$\tau = 105013.6 \text{ Pa}$$

K from Eq. (2.3.8):

$$K = 9.911 * 10^{-28}$$

Die constant G_{circle} from Eq. (6.1.3):

$$G_{circle} = \frac{\left(\frac{\pi}{4}\right)^{\frac{1}{5.956}} \cdot (5.08 * 10^{-3})^{\frac{3}{5.956}+1}}{2 * 0.1016}$$

$$= 1.678 * 10^{-3}$$

ΔP_0 with $\dot{Q} = 8.194 \cdot 10^{-5}$ m^3/s from Eq. (6.1.2):

$$\Delta P_0 = \frac{10^{-5} * (8.194 * 10^{-5})^{\frac{1}{5.956}}}{(9.911 * 10^{-28})^{\frac{1}{5.956}} \cdot 1.678 * 10^{-3}} = 42 \text{ bar}$$

b) Adiabatic flow

The relationship for the ratio $\dfrac{\Delta P}{\Delta P_0}$ is [17]

$$\frac{\Delta P}{\Delta P_0} = \frac{\ln \varkappa_L}{\varkappa_L - 1} \tag{6.3.1}$$

where

$$\varkappa_L = 1 + \frac{\beta \cdot \Delta P_0}{\varrho_m \cdot c_{pm}} \tag{6.3.2}$$

Temperature rise from Eq. (6.1.18):

$$\Delta T = \frac{\Delta P_0}{10 \cdot \varrho_m \cdot c_{pm}}$$

$$\Delta T = \frac{42}{10 * 1.12 * 1.6} = 2.34 \text{ K.}$$

For polystyrene

$$\beta = 0.026 \text{ K}^{-1}$$

$$\varkappa_L = 2.34 * 0.026 = 1.061$$

Finally ΔP from Eq. (6.3.1):

$$\Delta P = \Delta P_0 \cdot \frac{\ln \varkappa}{\varkappa_L - 1} = \frac{42 * \ln 1.061}{0.061}$$

$$= 40.77 \text{ bar}$$

In the adiabatic case the pressure drop is less because the dissipated heat is retained in the melt.

6.3.2   Mold Filling

As already mentioned the mold filling process was treated extensively in the programs [15], and [16] and recently by BANGERT [18]. In the following sections the more transparent method of STEVENSON [19] is given with an example.

6.3.2.1   Injection Pressure and Clamp Force

To determine the size of an injection molding machine in order to produce a given part, knowledge of the clamp force exerted by the mold is important, as this force should not exceed the clamp force of the machine.

6.3.2.1.1   Injection Pressure

The isothermal pressure drop for a disc-shaped cavity is given as [19]

$$\Delta p_1 = \frac{K_r}{10^5(1-n_R)}\left[\frac{360 \cdot \dot{Q} \cdot (1+2 \cdot n_R)}{N \cdot \theta \cdot 4\pi \cdot n_R \cdot r_2 \cdot b^2}\right]^{n_R} \cdot \left(\frac{r_2}{b}\right) \tag{6.3.3}$$

The fill time τ is defined as [19]

$$\tau = \frac{V \cdot a}{\dot{Q} \cdot b^2} \tag{6.3.4}$$

The Brinkman number is given by [19]

$$Br = \frac{b^2 \cdot K_r}{10^4 \cdot \lambda \cdot (T_M - T_W)} \cdot \left[\frac{\dot{Q} \cdot 360}{N \cdot \theta \cdot 2\pi \cdot b^2 \cdot r_2}\right]^{(1+n_R)} \tag{6.3.5}$$

Example with symbols and units:

Given data:
The material is ABS with $n_R = 0.2565$, which is the reciprocal of the power law exponent n. The constant K_r, which corresponds to the viscosity η_p is Eq. (6.2.31) is $K_r = 3.05 \cdot 10^4$.

Constant injection rate	$\dot{Q} = 160 \text{ cm}^3/\text{s}$
Part volume	$V = 160 \text{ cm}^3$
Half-thickness of the disc	$b = 2.1 \text{ mm}$
Radius of the disc	$r_2 = 120 \text{ mm}$
Number of gates	$N = 1$
Inlet melt temperature	$T_m = 518 \text{ K}$
Mold temperature	$T_W = 323 \text{ K}$
Thermal conductivity of the melt	$\lambda = 0.174 \text{ W/(m} \cdot \text{K)}$
Thermal diffusivity of the polymer	$a = 7.72 \cdot 10^{-4} \text{ cm}^2/\text{s}$
Melt flow angle [19]	$\theta = 360°$

The isothermal pressure drop in the mold Δp_1 is to be determined.

Solution:

Applying Eq. (6.3.3) for ΔP_1

$$\Delta p_1 = \frac{3.05 * 10^4}{10^5 (1 - 0.2655)} \left[\frac{360 * 160 * (1 + 2 * 0.2655)}{1 * 360 * 4\pi * 0.2655 * 12 * (0.105)^2} \right]^{0.2655} * \left(\frac{12}{0.105} \right)$$

$$= 254 \text{ bar}$$

Dimensionsless fill time τ from Eq. (6.3.4):

$$\tau = \frac{160 * 7.72 * 10^{-4}}{160 * (0.105)^2} = 0.07$$

Brinkman number from Eq. (6.3.5):

$$Br = \frac{0.105^2 * 3.05 * 10^4}{10^4 * 0.174 * 195} \left(\frac{160 * 360}{1 * 360 * 2\pi * (0.105)^2 * 12} \right)^{1.2655}$$

$$= 0.771$$

From the experimental results of STEVENSON [19] the following empirical relation was developed to calculate the actual pressure drop in the mold

$$\ln \left(\frac{\Delta P}{\Delta P_1} \right) = 0.337 + 4.7\tau - 0.093 \, Br - 2.6\tau \cdot Br \tag{6.3.6}$$

The actual pressure drop ΔP is therefore from Eq. (6.3.6):

$$\Delta P = 1.574 * \Delta P_1 = 1.574 * 254 = 400 \text{ bar}$$

6.3.2.1.2 Clamp Force

The calculation of clamp force is similar to that of the injection pressure. First the isothermal clamp force is determined from [19]

$$F_1(r_2) = 10 \cdot \pi r_2^2 \left(\frac{1 - n_R}{3 - n_R} \right) \cdot \Delta P_1 \tag{6.3.7}$$

where $F_1(r_2) = $ isothermal clamp force (N)

$F_1(r_2)$ for the example above is with Eq. (6.3.7)

$$F_1(r_2) = 10 * \pi * 12 * 12 * \left(\frac{1 - 0.2655}{3 - 0.2655} \right) * 254$$

$$= 308.64 \text{ kN}$$

The actual clamp force can be obtained from the following empirical relation, which was developed from the results published in [19].

$$\ln(F/F_1) = 0.372 + 7.6\,\tau - 0.084 \, Br - 3.538 \,\tau \cdot Br \tag{6.3.8}$$

Hence the actual clamp force F from Eq. (6.3.8)

$$F = 1.91 * 308.64 = 589.5 \, kN$$

The above relationships are valid for a disc-shaped cavity. Other geometries of the mold cavity can be taken into account on this basis in the manner described by STEVENSON [19].

6.3.3   Flowability of Injection-Molding Resins

The flowability of injection-molding materials can be determined on the basis of melt flow in a spiral channel. In practice a spiral-shaped mold of rectangular cross-section with the height and width in the order of a few millimeters is often used to classify the resins according to their flowability. The length L of the solidified plastic in the spiral is taken as a measure of the viscosity of the polymer concerned.

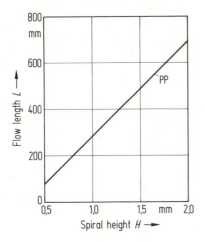

Fig. 6.10   Flow length L as a function of the spiral height H

Fig. 6.10 shows the experimentally determined flow length L as a function of the height H of the spiral for polypropylene. A quantitative relation between L and the parameters influencing L such as type of resin, melt temperature, mold temperature and injection pressure can be developed by using the dimensionless numbers as defined by THORNE [23] in the following manner:

The Reynolds number Re is given by [23]

$$Re = \frac{V_e^{(2-n_R)} \cdot \varrho \cdot H^{*n_R}}{k^*} \tag{6.3.9}$$

where

$$k^* = \eta_a \, \dot{\gamma}^{(1-n_R)} \tag{6.3.10}$$

$$V_e = \frac{\dot{Q}}{W \cdot H}$$

$$\dot{Q} = \frac{\dot{G}}{\varrho}$$

$$\dot{\gamma} = \frac{6 \cdot \dot{Q}}{W \cdot H^2}$$

$$H^* = 0.5 \cdot H$$

Prandtl number Pr [23]

$$Pr = \frac{k^* \cdot c_{\mathrm{p}} \cdot H^{*(1-n_{\mathrm{R}})}}{\lambda \cdot V_{\mathrm{e}}^{(1-n_{\mathrm{R}})}} \tag{6.3.11}$$

and Brinkman number Br [23]

$$Br = \frac{k^* \cdot V_{\mathrm{e}}^{(1+n_{\mathrm{R}})} \cdot H^{*(1-n_{\mathrm{R}})}}{\lambda \, (T_{\mathrm{M}} - T_{\mathrm{W}})} \tag{6.3.12}$$

In addition, the Graetz number is defined by

$$Gz = \frac{G \cdot c_{\mathrm{p}}}{\lambda \cdot L} \tag{6.3.13}$$

As shown in [20] and in Fig. 6.11 the Graetz number correlates well with the product $Re \cdot Pr \cdot Br$

$$Gz = f(Re \cdot Pr \cdot Br) \tag{6.3.14}$$

An explicit relationship for the spiral length L can therefore be computed from this correlation.

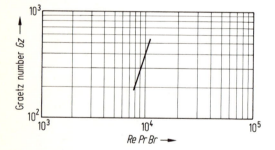

Fig. 6.11 Dimensionless groups for determining the flowability of a resin [20]

Symbols and units:

Br Brinkman number
c_{p} Specific heat kJ/(kg·K)
$\dot{\gamma}$ Apparent shear rate s^{-1}
G Mass flow rate kg/h
Gz Graetz number
H Height of the spiral mm
H^* Half-height of the spiral mm
k^* Constant from Eq. (6.3.10)
L Length of the spiral mm
n_{r} Reciprocal of the power law exponent

Pr Prandtl number
$\dot{Q}$ Volume flow rate m^3/s
Re Reynolds number
T_M Melt temperature °C
T_W Mold temperature °C
V_e Velocity of the melt front m/s
W Width of the spiral mm
λ Thermal conductivity $W/(m \cdot K)$
ϱ Melt density g/cm^3
η_a Melt viscosity $Pa \cdot s$

Example:

This example illustrates the calculation of the dimensionless numbers Gz, Re, Pr and Br for the given data:

$W = 10$ mm; $H = 2$ mm; $L = 420$ mm; $\varrho = 1.06$ g/cm^3; $c_p = 2$ $kJ/(kg \cdot K)$;

$\lambda = 1.5$ $W/(m \cdot K)$; $T_M = 270$ °C; $T_W = 70$ °C; $G = 211.5$ kg/h:

Resin-dependent constants according to Eq. (2.3.18):

$A_0 = 4.7649$; $A_1 = -0.4743$; $A_2 = -0.2338$; $A_3 = 0.081$
$A_4 = -0.01063$; $c_1 = 4.45$; $c_2 = 146.3$; $T_0 = 190$ °C;

Solution:

The conversion factors for the units used in the calculation of the dimensionless numbers below are

$F_1 = 0.001$; $F_2 = 1000$; $F_3 = 3600$;

The Graetz number Gz is calculated from

$$Gz = \frac{F_2 \cdot G \cdot c_p}{F_1 \cdot F_3 \cdot \lambda \cdot L}$$

with G in kg/h and L in mm.

From the above data $Gz = 186.51$

The Reynolds number is obtained from

$$Re = \frac{F_2 \cdot V_e^{(2-n_R)} \cdot \varrho \cdot H^{*n_R}}{k^*}$$

with V_e in m/s, H^* in m and ϱ in g/cm^3

From the given values $Re = 0.03791$

With H^* in m and V_e in m/s we get from

$$Pr = \frac{F_2 \cdot k^* \cdot c_p \cdot H^{*(1-n_R)}}{\lambda \cdot V_e^{(1-n_R)}}$$

$$Pr = 103\,302.87$$

and the Brinkman number Br from

$$Br = \frac{k^* \cdot V_e^{(1+n_r)} \cdot H^{*(1-n_r)}}{\lambda \cdot (T_M - T_W)}$$

$$Br = 1.9833$$

Finally the product $Re \cdot Pr \cdot Br$ is 7768.06.

6.3.4   Cooling of Melt in Mold

As mentioned in the Section 4.2.1 the numerical solution of the Fourier equation, Eq. (4.2.1) is presented here for crystalline and amorphous polymers.

6.3.4.1   Crystalline Polymers

It can be noticed from the enthalpy-temperature diagram of a crystalline polymer that there is a sharp enthalpy rise in the temperature region where the polymer begins to melt. This is due to the latent heat of fusion absorbed by the polymer when it is heated and has to be taken into account while calculating cooling curves of crystalline polymers.

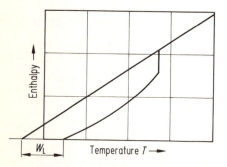

Fig. 6.12   Representation of temperature correction for latent heat [22]

By defining an equivalent temperature for the latent heat (Fig. 6.12) Gloor [22] calculated the temperature of a slab using the Fourier equation for the unsteady-state heat conduction. The numerical solution of Eq. (4.2.1) using the correction introduced by Gloor [22] was given in the work [25] on the basis of the method of differences after Schmidt [24]. A computer program for this solution is presented in [3]. The time interval used in this method is

$$\Delta t = \frac{c_p \cdot \varrho}{\lambda} \cdot \frac{\Delta x^2}{M} \tag{6.3.15}$$

where $\Delta t =$ time interval
$\Delta x =$ thickness of a layer
$M =$ number of layers, into which the slab is devided, beginning from the mid-plane of the slab (Fig. 6.13)

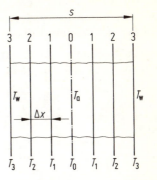

Fig. 6.13 Nomenclature for numerical solution of unsteady-state conduction in a slab [25]

The mold temperature and the thermodynamic properties of the polymer are assumed to be constant during the cooling process. The temperature, at which the latent heat is evolved and the temperature correction W_L (Fig. 6.12) are obtained from the enthalpy diagram as suggested by GLOOR [22]. An arbitrary difference of about 6 °C is assigned between the temperature of latent heat release at the mid-plane and the temperature at the outer surface of the slab.

Fig. 6.14 shows a sample plot of temperature as a function of time for a crystalline polymer.

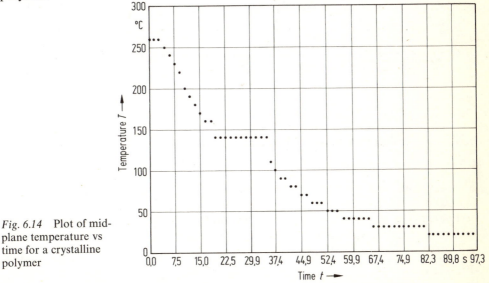

Fig. 6.14 Plot of mid-plane temperature vs time for a crystalline polymer

6.3.4.2   Amorphous Polymers

Amorphous polymers do not exhibit the sharp enthalpy change while passing from liquid to solid as crystalline plastics do. Consequently, when applying the numerical method of SCHMIDT [24] the correction for the latent heat can be left out in the calculation. A sample plot calculated with the computer program given in [3] is shown in Fig. 6.15 for amorphous polymers.

It is to be mentioned here that the analytical solutions for unsteady heat conduction given in Section 4.2.1 serve as good approximations for crystalline as well as amorphous polymers.

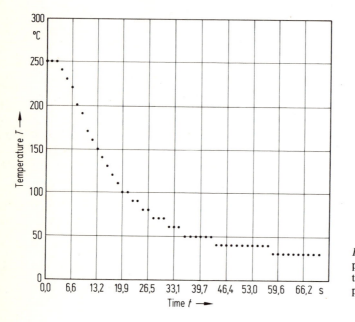

Fig. 6.15 Plot of midplane temperature vs time for an amorphous polymer

6.3.5   Design of Cooling Channels

6.3.5.1   Thermal Design

In practice the temperature of the mold wall is not constant, as it is influenced by the heat transfer between the melt and the cooling water. Therefore the geometry of the cooling channel lay-out, thermal conductivity of the mold material and velocity of cooling water affect the cooling time significantly.

The heat transferred from the melt to the cooling medium can be expressed as (Fig. 6.16)

$$Q_{ab} = 10^{-3} \cdot [(T_M - T_E) \, c_{ps} + i_m] \cdot \varrho_m \cdot \frac{s}{2} \cdot x \quad (kJ/m) \qquad (6.3.16)$$

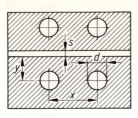

Fig. 6.16 Geometry for the thermal design of cooling channels

The heat received by the cooling water in the time t_K amounts to

$$Q_w = 10^{-3} \cdot t_K \left(\frac{1}{\lambda_{st} S_e} + \frac{1}{\alpha \cdot 10^{-3} \cdot 2 \cdot \pi \cdot R} \right)^{-1} *$$

$$* (T_W - T_{water}) \quad (kJ/m) \tag{6.3.17}$$

The cooling time t_K in this equation can be obtained from Eq. (4.2.11). The influence of the cooling channel lay-out on heat conduction can be taken into account by the shape factor S_e according to [23], [26].

$$S_e = \frac{2\pi}{\ln \left[\frac{2 \cdot X \cdot \sinh \left(\frac{2\pi y}{x} \right)}{\pi d} \right]} \tag{6.3.18}$$

With the values for the properties of water

$$c_p = 4.18 \text{ kJ/(kg} \cdot \text{K)}$$

$$\mu = 1.12 \times 10^{-3} \text{ Pa} \cdot \text{s}$$

$$\lambda = 0.6 \text{ W/(m} \cdot \text{K)}$$

the heat transfer coefficient α can be obtained from Eq. (4.5.2)

$$\alpha = \frac{0.031395}{d} \cdot Re^{0.8} \tag{6.3.19}$$

The mold temperature T_w in Eq. (4.2.11) is calculated iteratively from the heat balance $\dot{Q}_{ab} = \dot{Q}_w$.

Example with symbols and units:

Part thickness	$s = 2$ mm
Distance	$x = 30$ mm
Distance	$y = 10$ mm
Diameter of cooling channel	$d = 10$ mm
Melt temperature	$T_M = 250$ °C
Demolding temperature	$T_E = 90$ °C
Latent heat of fusion of the polymer	$i_m = 130$ kJ/kg
Specific heat of the polymer	$c_{ps} = 2.5$ kJ/(kg·K)

Melt density $\varrho_m = 0.79$ g/cm^3
Thermal diffusivity of the melt $a = 8.3 \times 10^{-4}$ cm^2/s
Kinematic viscosity of cooling water $v = 1.2 \times 10^{-6}$ m^2/s
Velocity of cooling water $u = 1$ m/s
Temperature of cooling water $T_{water} = 15$ °C
Thermal conductivity of mold steel $\lambda_{st} = 45$ W/(m·K)

With the data above the heat removed from the melt Q_{ab} according to Eq. (6.3.16) is

$$Q_{ab} = 10^{-3}[(250-90)*2.5+130]*0.79*\frac{2}{2}*30$$

$$= 12.56 \text{ kJ/m}$$

Shape factor S_e from Eq. (6.3.18):

$$S_e = \frac{2\pi}{\ln\left[\dfrac{2*30 \sinh\left(\dfrac{2\pi*10}{30}\right)}{\pi*10}\right]} = 3.091$$

Reynolds number of water:

$$Re = 10^{-3} \cdot u \cdot d/v$$

$$= \frac{10^{-3} \cdot 1 \cdot 10}{1.2 * 10^{-6}} = 8333$$

Using Eq. (6.3.19) the heat-transfer coefficient α

$$\alpha_{water} = \frac{0.031395 * Re^{0.8}}{10^{-3} * 10} = 4300 \text{ W/(m}^2 \cdot \text{K)}$$

From Eq. (6.3.17) we get for the heat received by the cooling water Q_w

$$Q_w = 10^{-3} \cdot t_K \left(\frac{1}{45*3.091} + \frac{1}{4300*10^{-3}*2\pi*5}\right)^{-1}$$

$$*(T_w - 15)$$

Cooling time t_K from Eq. (4.2.11):

$$t_K = \frac{(10^{-1}*2)^2}{\pi^2 * 8.3 * 10^{-4}} \cdot \ln\left[\frac{4}{\pi} \cdot \frac{(250 - T_w)}{(90 - T_w)}\right]$$

From the heat balance

$$Q_{ab} = Q_w = 12.56$$

we obtain by iteration

$$T_w = 37.83 \text{ °C}$$

Finally, the cooling time t_K with $T_w = 37.83$ is from Eq. (4.2.11)

$$t_K = 8.03 \text{ s}$$

The influence of the cooling channel lay-out on cooling time can be simulated on the basis of the equations given by changing the distances x and y (Fig. 6.16) as shown in Figs. 6.17 and 6.18. The effects of the temperature of cooling water and of its velocity are presented in Figs. 6.19 and 6.20 respectively. From these results it follows that the cooling time is significantly determined by the cooling channel lay-out.

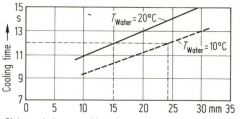

Fig. 6.17   Effect of cooling channel distance Y on cooling time

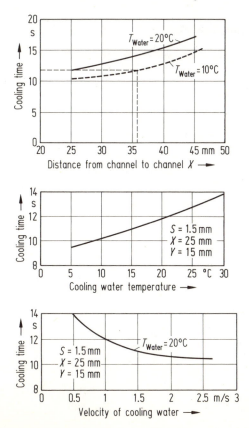

Fig. 6.18   Effect of cooling channel distance X on cooling time

Fig. 6.19   Influence of the temperature of cooling water on cooling time

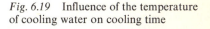

Fig. 6.20   Influence of the velocity of cooling water on cooling time

6.3.5.2   Mechanical Design

The cooling channels should be as close to the surface of the mold as possible so that heat can flow out of the melt in the shortest time possible.

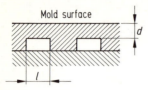

Fig. 6.21   Geometry for the mechanical design of cooling channels

However, the strength of the mold material sets a limit to the distance between the cooling channel and the mold surface. The allowable distance d (Fig. 6.21) taking the strength of the mold material into account was calculated by [27] on the basis of the following equations:

$$\sigma_{b_{max}} = \frac{0.5 \cdot P \cdot l^2}{d^2} \tag{6.3.20}$$

$$\tau_{max} = \frac{0.75 \cdot P \cdot l}{d} \tag{6.3.21}$$

$$f_{max} = \frac{1000 * P \cdot l^2}{d} \left(\frac{l^2}{32 \cdot E \cdot d^2} + \frac{0.15}{G} \right) \tag{6.3.22}$$

where p = mold pressure N/mm^2
   l, d = distances mm, see Fig. 6.21
   E = tensile modulus N/mm^2
   G = shear modulus N/mm^2
   $\sigma_{b_{max}}$ = allowable tensile stress N/mm^2
   τ_{max} = allowable shear stress N/mm^2
   f_{max} = maximum deflection of the mold material above the cooling
       channel μm

The minimisation of the distance d such that the conditions

$$f \leqq f_{max}$$

$$\sigma_b \leqq \sigma_{b_{max}}$$

$$\tau \leqq \tau_{max}$$

are satisfied, can be accomplished by the computer program given in [3]. The results of a sample calculation are shown Table 6.1.

The equations given are approximately valid for circular channels as well. The distance from wall to wall of the channel should roughly be around the channel length l or channel diameter considering from standpoint of the strength of mold material.

Table 6.1   Results of optimization of cooling channel distance in Fig. 6.21

Input		Output	
mold pressure	$P = 4.9 \text{ N/mm}^2$	channel distance	$d = 2.492 \text{ mm}$
maximum deflection	$f_{max} = 2.5 \text{ } \mu\text{m}$	deflection	$f = 2.487 \text{ } \mu\text{m}$
modulus of elasticity	$E = 70\,588 \text{ N/mm}^2$	tensile stress	$\sigma = 39.44 \text{ N/mm}^2$
modulus of shear	$G = 27\,147 \text{ N/mm}^2$	shear stress	$\tau = 14.75 \text{ N/mm}^2$
allowable tensile stress	$\sigma_{b_{max}} = 421.56 \text{ N/mm}^2$		
allowable shear stress	$\tau_{max} = 294.1 \text{ N/mm}^2$		
channel dimension	$l = 10 \text{ mm}$		

6.3.6   Melting in Injection Molding Screws

The plastication of solids in the reciprocating screw of an injection molding machine is a batch process and consists of two phases. During the stationary phase of the screw melting takes place mainly by conduction heating from the barrel. The melting during screw rotation time of the molding cycle is similar to that in an extrusion screw but instationary. At long times of screw rotation it approaches the steady-state condition of extrusion melting.

6.3.6.1   Melting by Heat Conduction

According to DONOVAN [28] the equation describing conduction melting can be written as

$$K = \frac{-2 \cdot 10^{-6}}{i \cdot \varrho_m} \left\{ \frac{(T_m - T_b) \cdot \lambda_m \cdot \exp(-K^2/4 \cdot \alpha_m)}{\sqrt{\pi \cdot a_m} \cdot erf(K/2\sqrt{a})} - \frac{(T_r - T_m) \cdot \lambda_s \cdot \exp(-K^2/a_s)}{\sqrt{\pi \cdot a_s} \cdot erfc(K/2\sqrt{a_s})} \right\} \quad (6.3.23)$$

where T = temperature °C

λ = thermal conductivity W/(m · K)

K = Parameter defined by [28] m/$\sqrt{\text{s}}$

a = thermal diffusivity m^2/s

i = latent heat of fusion kJ/kg

ϱ = density g/cm^3

Indices:

r: middle of solid bed

s: solid

m: melt

b: barrel

The parameter K can be determined iteratively by means of the computer program given in [9].

6.3.6.2   Melting during Screw Rotation

Analogous to the melting model of Tadmor (Section 6.2.3) DONOVAN [28] defines an area ratio A^*

$$A^* = \frac{A_s}{A_T}$$

to describe the melting or solid bed profile of a reciprocating screw quantitatively. A^* is the ratio of the cross-sectional area of solid bed A_s to the cross-sectional area of screw channel A_T.

The equations according to DONOVAN [28] for calculating the solid bed profiles are as follows:

$$A_f^* - A_i^* = A_f^* \left[K \sqrt{t_T - t_R + \left(\frac{\delta_i^2}{K^2} \right)} - \delta_i \right] \Big/ H \tag{6.3.24}$$

$$A_f^* = A_e^* - \left[\frac{(A_f^* - A_i^*)}{\left[1 - \exp\left(\frac{-\beta \cdot 2\pi \cdot N \cdot t_R}{60} \right) \right]} \right] * \tag{6.3.25}$$

$$* \exp(-\beta \cdot 2\pi \cdot N \cdot t_R / 60)$$

$$A_i^* = A_e^* - \left[\frac{(A_f^* - A_i^*)}{\left[1 - \exp\left(\frac{-\beta \cdot 2\pi \cdot N \cdot t_R}{60} \right) \right]} \right] * \tag{6.3.26}$$

$$* \exp\left(-\frac{\beta \cdot 2\pi \cdot N \cdot t_R}{60} \right)$$

where t = total cycle time s
t_R = screw rotation time s
δ_i = thickness of melt film m
H = depth of the screw channel m
β = dimensionless parameter
N = screw speed rpm

Indices

i: beginning of screw rotation
f: end of screw rotation
e: extrusion

The thickness of the melt film δ_i and the solid bed profile for steady-state extrusion A_e^* can be obtained from the relationships in the Tadmor model given in Section 6.2.3.

The area ratio at the start of screw rotation A_i^* and the value at the end of screw rotation A_f^* can then be obtained by using the computer program given

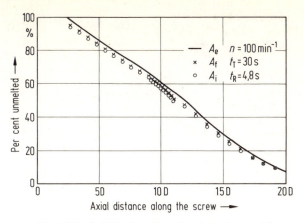

Fig. 6.22   Solid bed profile of an injection molding screw

in [9]. Fig. 6.22 shows the solid bed profiles of a computer simulation [9] for a particular resin at given operating conditions.

Literature

[1] RAO, N.: EDV-Auslegung von Extrudierwerkzeugen, Kunststoffe 69 (1979) 3, p. 226

[2] PROCTER, B.: SPE J. 28 (1972) p. 34

[3] RAO, N.: Designing Machines and Dies for Polymer Processing with Computer Programs, Hanser, Munich (1981)

[4] RAMSTEINER, F.: Kunststoffe 61 (1971) 12, p. 943

[5] SCHENKEL, G.: Private Communication

[6] TADMOR, Z., KLEIN, I.: Engineering Principles of Plasticating Extrusion, Van Nostrand Reinhold, New York (1970)

[7] BERNHARDT, E.C.: Processing of Thermoplastic Materials, Reinhold, New York (1963)

[8] RAUWENDAAL, C.: Polymer Extrusion, Hanser, Munich (1986)

[9] RAO, N.: Computer Aided Design of Plasticating Screws, Programs in Fortran and Basic, Hanser, Munich (1986)

[10] KLEIN, I., MARSHALL, D.I.: Computer Programs for Plastics Engineers, Reinhold, New York (1968)

[11] WOOD, S.D.: SPE 35, Antec (1977)

[12] SQUIRES, P.H.: SPE-J. 16 (1960), p. 267

[13] PEARSON, J.R.A.: Reports of University of Cambridge, Polymer Processing Research Centre (1969)

[14] JOHANNABER, F.: Injection Molding Machines, Hanser, Munich (1983)

[16] CADMOULD: Project Rechnergestützte Formteil und Werkzeugauslegung, IKV, Aachen

[17] MCKELVEY, J.M.: Polymer Processing, John Wiley & Sons, New York (1962)

[18] BANGERT, H.: Systematische Konstruktion von Spritzgießwerkzeugen unter Rechnereinsatz, Dissertation, RWTH Aachen (1981)

[19] STEVENSON, J.F.: Polymer Engineering and Science 18 (1978) p. 573

[20] RAO, N.: Kunststoffe 73 (1983) 11, p. 696

[21] RAO, N., HAGEN, K., KRÄMER, A.: Kunststoffe 69 (1979) 10, p. 173

[22] GLOOR, W.E.: Heat Transfer Calculations, Technical Papers, Volume IX-I, p. 1

[23] THRONE, J.L.: Plastics Process Engineering, Marcel Dekker Inc. New York (1979)

[24] SCHMIDT, E.: Einführung in die Technische Thermodynamik, Springer, Berlin (1962) p. 353
[25] MENGES, G., JÜRGENS, W.: Plastverarbeiter 19 (1968) p. 201
[26] VDI-Wärmeatlas, VDI-Verlag, Düsseldorf (1984)
[27] LINDNER, E.: Berechenbarkeit von Spritzgießwerkzeugen, VDI-Verlag, Düsseldorf (1974) p. 109
[28] DONOVAN, R.C.: Polymer Engineering and Science 11 (1971) p. 361
[29] SCHENKEL, G.: Kunststoff-Extrudiertechnik. Hanser, Munich (1963)
[30] FENNER, R.T.: Extruder Screw Design. ILiFFE Books, London (1970)
[31] FISCHER, P.: Dissertation, RWTH Aachen (1976)
[32] POTENTE, H.: Proceedings, 9. Kunststofftechnisches Kolloquium, IKV, Aachen (1978)

A Final Word

The aim of this book is to present the basic formulas of rheology, thermodynamics, heat transfer and strength of materials applicable to plastics engineering and to show how, starting from these formulas, models for designing polymer processing equipment can be developed.

Thoroughly worked-out examples in metric units illustrate the use of these formulas, which have been successfully applied by well-known machine manufacturers time and again in their design work. However, owing to the ever-increasing growth of knowledge brought forth by research and development in the plastics field a book of this kind needs to be renewed often and as such cannot claim to be an exhaustive work.

Index